BY ANTHONY RIZZUTO
Foreword by Quentin Anderson

Camus' Imperial Vision

SOUTHERN ILLINOIS
UNIVERSITY PRESS

Carbondale and Edwardsville

ALL RIGHTS RESERVED
Printed in the United States of America
Edited by Dan Seiters
Designed by Bob Nance, Design for Publishing
Production supervised by Richard Neal

Works by Albert Camus
quoted with permission from Editions Gallimard.

This book is lovingly dedicated to my wife, *DORA*.

Contents

Foreword

By Quentin Anderson

In this trenchant book Anthony Rizzuto traces the path, brilliant as a comet's arc, along which Camus moved from the desolate isolation of *L'Etranger* to the embrace of the human condition in *L'Homme Révolté*, *La Chute*, and succeeding works. Its stages are marked by quotations from notebooks, novels, and stories that have an undiminished power to shock us into awareness: "Quand on n'a pas de caractère il faut bien se donner une méthode"—which comes close to being an epigraph for the intellectual behavior of the 1980s. Rizzuto never allows us to forget that we are dealing with an artist who earned such clarity as this through an unremitting struggle with himself. Camus never bared his soul or took intellectual holidays. Only by setting himself at a remove from us could he make us privy to states of the human spirit that seem as remote as the stars—or as the godhead to which he originally aspired. What in the end Camus wished to represent was, Rizzuto tells us, "the broken and cumulative curves of a man's inhabited life." In no other man of the writer's period does exquisitely executed imaginative accomplishment so closely follow the movement of public events, while at the same time rigorously preserving that space which enables reasoned reflection and representation.

This book makes it abundantly clear that it was Camus' original intellectual and emotional horizon that prepared him for membership in the Communist party and that this in turn was the basis for his realization that the relation between abstraction and aggression he found in himself was continuous with the abstraction and aggression manifested in totalitarian parties and states. Camus' return upon himself, his repossession not only of his past, but of the very idea that he had a past, led him to say, "Jouir de soi est impossible; je le sais, malgré les grands dons qui sont les miens pour cet exercice," and to go on to demonstrate the claim to imperial vision inherent in the politics of Sartre and others.

The man who made these things plain in the 1950s committed the grossest impiety many people were able to imagine. An attack on their collective hope, no matter how outrageous the behavior of the country entrusted with its realization, was felt as an attack on the very selfhood of those who followed Stalin, who clung to the conviction that one must not attack the vessel of collective hope even though it was filled with blood.

The cloud which thereafter obscured Camus' fame resulted from this impiety: his equation of impersonality with violence. It was a cloud that covered others, and led, for example, to attacks on George Orwell in England and Lionel Trilling in the United States. The assertion that the freedom of individual minds depended upon their granting a like freedom to others became an offense against the collective hope. Yet as our times ever more insistently demonstrate the connection between terrorism and abstraction, Camus' uniquely cogent representation of the impulse to violence which characterizes intellectual imperialism takes on ever more force. Rizzuto offers excellent grounds for admiring the writer who at once plumbed himself and his times; he has in doing so issued a sharp warning to his countrymen.

Acknowledgments

A book is a collective as well as an individual enterprise. Raymond Gay-Crosier, Paul Viallaneix, Germaine Brée, and Quentin Anderson are teachers and authors who have set the finest examples of scholarship and I wish to acknowledge the help and encouragement they willingly gave to me.

I have also been fortunate here at the State University of New York at Stony Brook in having three friends and colleagues, Mark Whitney, Frederick Brown, and Carol Blum, who read the manuscript in various stages of preparation and who offered their invaluable comments and criticisms. They deserve more thanks than I can express.

Finally, special mention must be made of the late Francine Camus who so graciously permitted me to read the manuscript of Camus' unfinished novel, *Le Premier homme*.

Note on Abbreviations

The sources from which I have quoted most frequently are abbreviated as follows:

TRN   Camus, Albert. *Théâtre, Récits, Nouvelles.* Roger Quilliot, ed. Bruges: Gallimard, 1962.

E   Camus, Albert. *Essais.* Roger Quilliot and L. Faucon, eds. Bruges: Gallimard, 1965.

MH   Camus, Albert. *La Mort heureuse, Cahiers Albert Camus, 1,* Jean Sarocci, ed. Paris: Gallimard, 1971.

PC   Viallaneix, Paul. *Le Premier Camus,* suivi de *Ecrits de jeunesse d'Albert Camus, Cahiers Albert Camus,* 2, Mayenne: Gallimard, 1973.

C, 1   Camus, Albert. *Carnets,* mai 1935–février 1942. Paris: Gallimard, 1962.

C, 2   Camus, Albert. *Carnets,* janvier 1942–mars 1951. Paris: Gallimard, 1964.

Camus' Imperial Vision

1 / *The Imperial Vision*

CAMUS once reported that the highest praise a man could receive among workers in Algeria was to be called, quite simply, a man. "*C'est un homme*" meant specifically that you were a man of your word, that you demanded respect for your family and yourself and deserved that respect so long as you did not take unfair advantage of your physical or intellectual powers. In more general terms, manhood could only be achieved successfully within a nexus of human relationships. Having sketched this basic ethic in "Au Service de l'homme" (E, 1544–46), where he also named the proletariat as the sole, legitimate force for the renovation of Europe, Camus concluded: "Pour ma part, je ne vois pas que nous ayons besoin de plus."

What emerges from this article, written in 1944, only months before the Armistice, is not only the specifics of a worker's ethic but the evident pleasure Camus derives from the discovery, after four years of a global war, that there are any specifics left at all. Resistant and, in his own words, a voyager in hell, Camus is throwing lines back to his life as a poor boy in Algeria, "un passé de pauvreté et de vérité," and feels nourished again. Able to re-locate himself in a normal geographical and political space, he can reassure us that not everything had been lost. Values rooted in a specific class and in his own personal experiences still re-mained out of which a man could create a viable future. At this time, however, Camus was also writing *La Peste* and, though this war of wars was hell, he knew that there was another hell of his own devising, one that bore the unmistakable stamp of his most private self. Being a man and a worker directly in-volved with a family and a social class held some kind of key to a better world. But Camus, who once had asked: "Quand aurai-je le courage de ne plus être un homme?" (PC, 185); who had stated: "Je veux être indifférent" (PC, 188); and who, above all, had written *Caligula* (a portrait of a murderous emperor ide-alized as a young Nietzschean), also wanted to have nothing to do with this world and to create a private self so totally indepen-dent of the human condition as to usurp the prerogatives of a god. The war had devastated countless lives, and he too had preached indifference or misanthropic contempt, the dislimn-ing of persons. What characterizes this early period, according to Roger Quilliot, is Camus' "tentation de l'absolu,"[1] and, ac-cording to John Cruickshank, a "withdrawal from temporal ex-istence . . . into more speculative and timeless self-awareness."[2] It is equally evident, however, that this withdrawal from the col-lective life into pure self-absorption, whether it took the form of passive indifference or active aggression, was to be achieved through the systematic denial of the importance of human life.

In the recent history of Europe alone, many political events and literary traditions constituted a supportive framework for Camus' nihilism. The Reign of Terror, for example, undertook the destruction not only of the opponents of a newly established Republic but of the idea of opposition itself. Its goal was suc-cinctly defined by the revolutionary Saint-Just, prosecuting at-torney for the condemnation of Louis XVI: "L'établissement de la République est la destruction de tout ce qui n'est pas elle."

1. *La Mer et les prisons* (Paris: Gallimard, 1970), pp. 77–78.
2. *Albert Camus and the Literature of Revolt* (New York: Oxford University Press, 1959), p. 159.

The figure of Saint-Just will loom large in Camus' *L'Homme révolté*, a study of the nihilist tradition in Europe and an investigation of the many sources of his own radical convictions: Sade's philosophy of blind instinct, which divides the human race into the "strong" and the "weak"; the romantic doctrine of individualism, which declares the self to be sole source of its happiness; Hegel's view that the essential human relationship is that of master and slave, a view in turn adopted by the Marxists to describe the class war; Nietzsche's "superman" reincarnated in the heroes of Gide and Malraux, authors who exercised a profound influence on Camus; symbolist narcissism that would organize all human energies into self-contemplation and self-love; the surrealist notion of immediate gratification. Events in his own adult life forced Camus to face the concrete results of nihilism: the advent of Hitler and Nazism, which mobilized sympathetic responses and active collaboration from the extreme political right, and of Stalin whose purges and concentration camps in the forties and fifties could boast at the very least the tacit tolerance of most of the political left.

Although World War II pitted democratic forces against Nazi Germany, it was becoming evident to Camus that the enemy was not an altogether alien menace, that the imperialist claim to supreme power was not an isolated aberration of the twentieth century but a variant in a long European tradition that had become morally and intellectually respectable. Rachel Bespaloff summarized the conflict in Camus and his generation between dreams of omnipotence and the decision to join the fight against nazism. "Le drame de cette génération nietzschéenne," she writes, "c'est qu'elle ait exalté la volonté de puissance dans l'individu au moment où elle s'apprêtait à la combattre au dehors sous la forme de l'impérialisme."[3] Part of the credit Camus will always enjoy among readers, perhaps more than any other modern French writer and certainly more than Sartre, stems from his willingness to investigate that contradiction without equivocation.

In Algeria Camus committed himself to political reforms as a journalist, member of the Communist party, and director of

3. "Le Monde du condamné à mort," *Esprit*, no. 163 (January 1950), p. 3.

a worker's theater. He spoke often of human ties and the responsibilities they impose, and he himself enjoyed the camaraderie of sports, activist politics, and the rehearsals and performances of plays. Camus warns that we have lost the habit of studying people's faces: "Nous ne regardons plus nos contemporains" (C, 1, 70), suggesting that we prefer easy judgments and their abstractions to the complex analyses of character; he knows that the benefits obtained from society also require sacrifices: "Il est normal de donner un peu de sa vie pour ne pas la perdre tout entière" (C, 1, 97); and he makes this shrewd assessment of the loner's duplicity: "Celui qui se veut le plus solitaire et anarchiste est encore celui qui brûle le plus de paraître aux yeux du monde. Ce qui compte ce sont les hommes" (PC, 287). The autobiographical essays in *L'Envers et l'endroit*, which deal in large part with a son's ambivalent relationship with his mother, also demonstrate Camus' ability to convey to his reader the complexities of a private, domestic situation.

He tells us that his mother suffered ill health, that she seldom spoke and was partially deaf. We also learn that Camus' father was killed at the battle of the Marne in World War I, when Camus was six months old. He asks himself whether or not he loves his mother, his sole surviving parent, and his question leads to another, the same one but in reverse, whether or not she loves him. Evidently, she never said she did. The questions remain unanswered, the dilemma unresolved because of what Camus perceives to be his mother's most characteristic trait, her apparent indifference to her son. It is "apparent" because, in Camus' view, either she felt no love, or else her love was so absolute that it transcended speech and other forms of demonstration. Camus also observes that same indifference within himself. Unable to say whether it, too, derives from emotional emptiness or plenitude, he does understand that it allows him at times to disregard and neglect a woman whose nature, nevertheless, he shares intimately.

Camus, however, just as often turned away from these populated crises in order to move closer to an inward scene where he alone performed. Such solitude at times was the result of circumstances and therefore temporary; more often it was the result of efforts to eliminate all distractions, particularly people, and to extend one man's soliloquy over an entire lifetime. Germaine Brée, in what remains one of the best introductions to Camus' thought, detected in *L'Envers et l'endroit* "a surge of love and detachment."[4] That detachment, however, that perspective through which a writer observes and investigates reality, through which he may enter the subjectivity of others, is changing into indifference or aggression, the desire to remain one. Camus is reserving for his fiction and formal essays the innermost, secret part of himself.

The reader confronts a series of assertions that challenge and often quite overwhelm the very notion of commitment in any of its forms. At first such assertions are not presented systematically. As early as 1932 and 1933 Camus writes that God is God because he does not know himself (PC, 183); that he himself wants to be indifferent (PC, 188); and that art presents one method for achieving divine status (PC, 251). From 1935 on, the *Carnets*, Camus' private notebooks, begin to pursue these matters with increasing frequency and with greater precision: "Je ne sais pas ce que je pourrais souhaiter de mieux que cette continuelle présence de moi-même à moi-même" (C, 1, 23); "Je veux tenir ma vie entre mes mains" (C, 1, 75). Camus demonstrated often enough, particularly as a journalist in "Misère de la Kabylie," eleven articles devoted to the 1939 famine in North Africa, his knowledge of the economic realities, of the compromises that become necessary when politics are viewed not as the translation of a single ideal but as a difficult choice among confusing options. The impact of his journalistic work derives in part from the soundness of the proposals he offers for a given problem but even more from his clear sense of our organic relationship to people and institutions. He sees himself in these articles as a participant in a world that is plural.

If, on the other hand, the self were to become coherent once and for all, its free nature fixed outside time's changes, and secure in the undiscouraged luxury of its perfection, capable, in other words, of being held in one's hands, it would enjoy imperial status. It would be a fiction. The birth of an imperial self, henceforth, owing nothing to flesh, less a birth than a lucid deci-

4. *Camus*, rev. ed. (New Brunswick: Rutgers University Press, 1972), p. 79.

sion of the will, would be miraculous. To achieve this end, to abolish the past and all inner conflict, reality is transcended and in the process, as Camus very slowly discovered, destroyed.

Camus, of course, knew there is no absolute knowledge of that reality, no human identity susceptible to one single definition. In his student essay for the *Diplôme d'Etudes Supérieures* entitled *Métaphysique chrétienne et néoplatonisme*, he had already examined with more than scholarly interest, Plotinus' inquiry into the nature of self: "C'est ainsi qu'apparaît une conception du moi à première vue paradoxale, mais très féconde: 'Il n'y a pas un point où on puisse fixer ses propres limites, de manière à dire: Jusque-là c'est moi'" (E, 1282). Whether the self, like God, is limitless, and ethics irrelevant, whether it should accept limits from others or impose only its own, are questions that acquire a fierce urgency in Camus' major works. The climate of absolutism in *L'Etranger*, *La Peste*, *La Chute*, and in his plays threatens to become and often does become violent because the imperial vision that so many of the characters share with their author requires and receives the ultimate test, the translation of this vision of self into action, regardless of the human consequences.

The first formal expressions that Camus gives to his imperial vision and its conflict with a more conservative notion of an ethically and socially integrated self are found in a series of texts he wrote between 1937 and 1939.

In "Noces à Tipasa," for example, Camus tells us that in the spring Tipasa is inhabited by the gods and he proceeds to become a god. Beginning with "nous," a group travelling by bus to the shore, Camus quickly disassociates himself from those who would have "l'ordre et la mesure" (E, 56) and experiences freedom, "le grand libertinage de la nature et de la mer" (E, 56), "cette possession tumultueuse de l'onde par mes jambes" (E, 57). The purpose of this union is to release an inner nature equal temporarily to the boundless world it would espouse. That world is the ocean or the sky:

J'ouvre les yeux et mon coeur à la grandeur insoutenable de ce ciel gorgé de chaleur. Ce n'est pas si facile de devenir ce qu'on est, de retrouver sa mesure profonde. . . . J'apprenais à respirer, je m'intégrais et je m'accomplissais. Je gravissais l'un après l'autre des côteaux dont chacun me réservait une récompense, comme ce temple dont les colonnes mesurent la course du soleil. (E, 56)

"Mesure profonde" successfully assumes the challenge of "grandeur insoutenable" and in its triumph makes Camus' solar ascension the sign and proof of his divinity. What is most significant is that the integration Camus seeks here is with the nonhuman. Yet merging with the sea or sky does not lead to personal loss, a dispersal of self fractured by impersonal elements. "Absence d'horizon," (E, 57), for example, becomes an invitation to infinity, as the body's boundaries dissolve and disappear, in blue space or through a fluid exchange, only to reorganize themselves into a higher nature. This cycle of destruction and resurrection is acted out within one's self exclusively, independent of any social apparatus. There does remain the matter of time because the body's transcendental experience, as Camus admits, is temporary. His god is not immortal. Memory, however, is not allowed to play its role. Camus will have nothing to do with the remembrance of things past which might force unfavorable comparisons. The goal is to preserve the purity of one perfect moment. Similes are therefore excluded. Instead Camus stresses "oubli": "Il faudrait admirer que le monde nous paraisse nouveau pour avoir été seulement oublié" (E, 59). Oblivion allows experiences to be recreated because it cancels the past. The result is more miracle than reality. Each day will be the first day and Camus ends up speaking like Adam: "Je décris et je dis: 'Voici qui est rouge, qui est bleu, qui est vert. Ici est la mer, la montagne, les fleurs'" (E, 57).

Camus achieves an ideal expressed a few years earlier: "C'est moi-même que je trouve au fond de l'univers. . . . Tout à l'heure, d'autres choses et les hommes me reprendront. Mais laissez-moi découper cette minute dans l'étoffe du temps" (C, 1, 21). We see how Camus isolates that moment in Tipasa and makes himself believe, for a moment, that he is a god and that nothing else exists. Whatever happens, he makes happen.

The reader, however, is hardly offended. We respond fully to the lyrical beauty of these descriptions. Though Camus will certainly equal himself, he will never again write more beautifully.

We are not disturbed by the social implications of this lyricism because the world created in "Noces à Tipasa" is bracketed by silence. Camus is on vacation. The swimmer's glory is a privileged moment and under the sky's high dome there is ample room for privileged moments. There "l'ordre et la mesure" can be temporarily suspended. The disturbing power of Camus' lyricism manifests itself when that brief sensation of omnipotence threatens to become permanent.

The lyrical equation Camus sets up between himself and those elements in nature waiting to release his spirit is partially reproduced in *La Mort heureuse* and *Caligula*. The free exchange between self and nature, the basis of Camus' sensual beatitude, shifts to a different plane when nature is replaced by society. Patrice Mersault and Caligula try to achieve through other people what the young man in "Noces" achieved through the sea and the sky. These texts are experimental. The strong political bent in Camus' character evidently urged him to try to insert his solitude into social collectivities and to accomplish this feat without compromise.

The dilemma of Patrice Mersault in *La Mort heureuse* is the dilemma of money. Interpreting the proverb "Time is money" literally, he kills and robs his wealthy friend Zagreus and buys time. Because money is time, earning money slowly becomes synonymous with dying slowly, with a humiliating human condition. Wealth, on the other hand, grants Mersault independence and his avowed purpose is to eliminate from his life all those situations and people that dilute the attention he would give only to himself and, finally, to his death. Mersault wants to die with his eyes open. For an atheist, the desire to be god must eventually come to terms with human mortality because to be fully present, fully aware at the moment of death approximates total self-control. In one sense, Camus is transposing the shock he received when he was stricken with tuberculosis at the age of seventeen, when, at the height of his physical powers, he became conscious of his mortality. Mersault's crime, to this extent, organizes in literary terms Camus' rage against extinction.

The lucidity Mersault brings to his own death in effect cancels it because he is fully awake until the last moment. His death also becomes a suicide. It denies mortality by going it one better.

What started as rage ends up an ideal. Mersault resembles Caligula who knows in advance the conspirators will kill him and who screams out with his last breath: "Je suis encore vivant" (TRN, 108).

Just as the man who would be god flaunts his mortality, so does his lucidity exploit oblivion. In Part II entitled "La Mort consciente," Camus points up this crucial factor:

Mersault s'aperçut que pas une seule fois il n'avait songé à Zagreus comme à l'homme qu'il avait tué de ses mains. Il reconnut en lui cette faculté d'oubli qui n'appartient qu'à l'enfant, au génie et à l'innocent. Innocent, bouleversé par la joie, il comprit enfin qu'il était fait pour le bonheur. (MH, 125)

Whereas the swimmer forgot his experience in order to relive it, Mersault forgets his victim, not to create others, although he could conceivably do so, but in order to merit the epithet "innocent." The genius, apparently, is amoral and the child premoral. The innocent man, also, can kill with his hands and, unlike the rest of humanity, remain untouched by the event. Wealthy, Mersault can enjoy the benefits of a crime that for him never took place. Camus has created a situation where absolute innocence, an attribute in theory reserved for God, becomes inevitable. Working in a long literary tradition of the perfect crime or legal murder that includes *Crime and Punishment* and *Les Caves du Vatican*, Camus demonstrates how the codes of human behavior must not be circumvented hypocritically, but first disobeyed and then destroyed. Mersault is innocent because he forgets his crime and because he committed it.

La Mort heureuse was the study of a private life; *Caligula* is the study of a public one and the stakes are much higher. There were no people in "Noces à Tipasa," no politics, and consequently no blood. In *La Mort heureuse* Mersault succeeds in his quest for transcendence by killing one man. Caligula is tragic because the emperor exercises his power within a more complex society and because he fails.

Caligula appears on stage after the death of his young sister with whom he had had incestuous relations. Traumatized by this unexpected death, he consciously decides to transcend the human condition by incorporating into himself that which makes it human, namely death. He becomes a murderer. He will now inflict pain and try never again to feel pain. We could say that Caligula changes from a virtuous emperor into an evil emperor except that he would consider both adjectives inappropriate and irrelevant. He becomes an emperor, one who creates events. He is no longer a man who participates in them and who runs the risk of being victimized by them.

The ability to be reborn, to redefine oneself without biological prerequisites, purely out of one's will, replaces both psychology and religion with a kind of lay mysticism, a secular incarnation. This ability implies the power to destroy oneself as well. The signs of Caligula's absolute power are visible in the play, in the number of victims he creates, including himself:

Je vis, je tue, j'exerce le pouvoir délirant du destructeur, auprès de quoi celui du créateur paraît une singerie. C'est cela le bonheur, cette insupportable délivrance, cet universel mépris, le sang, la haine autour de moi, cet isolement nonpareil de l'homme qui tient toute sa vie sous son regard, la joie démesurée de l'assassin impuni, cette logique implacable qui broie des vies humaines . . . pour parfaire enfin la solitude éternelle que je désire. (TRN, 106)

As a man who holds his life within his field of vision, who can see his own beginning and end, Caligula, as in some unholy trinity, plays father, son, and grim reaper to his own life, creator and created, murderer and victim, a divine birth and a divine suicide.

The breakdown in Caligula occurs at the end when he strangles Caesonia while pretending to embrace her from behind. His older and maternal mistress, she is his final victim. It becomes apparent that all the victims lead to her and through her to him. After killing, as it were, the inhabitants of life, Caligula destroys the source of life itself, the only proof that something preceded Caligula's decision to become Caligula. The scene is powerful partly because it echoes a troubling event in Camus' personal life, the evening his mother was attacked by an unknown assailant:

Elle regardait alors passer les gens. Derrière elle, la nuit s'amassait peu
à peu. Devant elle, les magasins s'illuminaient brusquement. La rue se
grossissait de monde et de lumières. Elle s'y perdait dans une contemplation sans but. Le soir dont il s'agit, un homme avait surgi derrière elle, l'avait traînée, brutalisée et s'était enfui en entendant du
bruit. Elle n'avait rien vu, et s'était évanouie. (E, 26)

Camus was not present at the scene but he describes it as if he
were.[5] The night massed menacingly behind his mother becomes a man and that unknown man becomes Caligula, Camus'
advocate. Camus decided to have Caesonia, like his mother, attacked from behind and, at the same time, to make her much
older than Caligula, whom she calls a child, and whose every
whim she indulges. This play calls the ultimate question that
Camus avoided in *Noces* and *La Mort heureuse*: would a man, in
order to achieve divine solitude, kill his mother? Caligula does,
but when he kills Caesonia he immediately denounces himself
and his ambition. He expresses a remorse Mersault could never
express because, for one thing, Mersault had killed a man. In
part because Camus never knew his father, that murder simply
did not mobilize deep feelings in Camus. *La Mort heureuse* often
resembles a student's sketch of Nietzsche or Dostoevsky.

Camus, however, did not give up. He searched for a way to
have a character kill his mother without remorse. Only when the
man-god's disaffiliation from family and society, both useless to
his purpose, became literal would it be total. Camus tried again
in *L'Etranger*.

Meursault seldom refers to his past. He lives in his body, on
the level of sensation.

His awareness of nature and desire has the directness of an
uncomplicated physical contact. "J'avais envie de serrer son
épaule par-dessus sa robe. J'avais envie de ce tissu fin" (TRN,
1179); "Le bruit des premières vagues sous la plante des pieds,
l'entrée du corps dans l'eau" (TRN, 1180). Camus will remain
faithful to this positive element in Meursault, his ability to find

5. Alain Costes, *Albert Camus ou la parole manquante* (Paris: Payot, 1973), p. 71.

in his body both the source of his happiness and the vehicle for shaping it.

As a result of this simplicity, however, Meursault reacts to other people depending on whether or not they are present. It seems that this indifference applies to Meursault himself who, as Sartre pointed out, uses the "passé composé" to describe his life in terms of separate and unrelated particles of experience, a separate Meursault for each separate moment.[6] Not unlike a child, out of sight for Meursault means out of reach. Critics as diverse as Champigny, Barrier, and Fitch also agree that Meursault is describing the book's events after they have occurred.[7] We can add that the discontinuities are deliberate and that Meursault's seemingly colorless indifference is nevertheless dyed with purpose. In prison he admits that he learns to remember, to make connections, and to see a pattern in his own behavior, if for no other reason than to tell the priest and the reader: "J'avais toujours raison" (TRN, 1210).

Meursault is the author of a journal. He describes his life but, at the same time, deliberately mutes the organizing impulses of art so that the discontinuities and accidents of life fill the foreground. For reasons that we must explore, Meursault wishes to avoid, as he describes his life, at least the appearance of any cumulative effect or purposeful goal. As Cruickshank so aptly indicates, he wants to view his life as a succession of events, not a sequence.[8]

The event that leads to Meursault's condemnation is his mother's death. The telegram announcing her death opens *L'Etranger*. Similarly in the first entry of the *Carnets* Camus reflects on a mother's influence over her son's life. Both texts begin under the sign of the mother and in them Camus transcribes some of his most intimate feelings:

Ce que je veux dire:

6. "Explication de *L'Etranger*," *Situations*, 1 (Paris: Gallimard, 1947): 117–18.

7. Robert Champigny, *Sur un héros païen* (Paris: Gallimard, 1959), Maurice-George Barrier, *L'Art du récit dans L'Etranger* (Paris: Nizet, 1962), and Brian T. Fitch, *Narrateur et narration dans L'Etranger d'Albert Camus* (Paris: Lettres Modernes, 1960).

8. *Albert Camus and the Literature of Revolt*, p. 156.

Qu'on peut avoir—sans romantisme—la nostalgie d'une pauvreté per-
due. Une certaine somme d'années vécues misérablement suffisent à
construire une sensibilité. Dans ce cas particulier, le sentiment bizarre
que le fils porte à sa mère constitue *toute sa sensibilité*. Les manifestations
de cette sensibilité dans les domaines les plus divers s'expliquent suf-
fisamment par le souvenir latent, matériel de son enfance (une glu qui
s'accroche à l'âme).
De là, pour qui s'en aperçoit, une reconnaissance et donc une mauvaise conscience. De là encore et par comparaison, si l'on a changé de
milieu, le sentiment de richesses perdues. . . .
A mauvaise conscience, aveu nécessaire. L'oeuvre est un aveu, il me
faut témoigner. (C, 1, 15–16)

Camus expresses for his mother the opposite feelings of grati-
tude and guilt. The roots of that guilt are not too clearly explained except that it evidently has something to do with the
"memory" of a childhood past. If, as "et donc" suggests, a bad
conscience automatically follows "reconnaissance," then those
ties that bind a son to his mother must be both "recognized" and
despised, "une glu," as Camus puts it. Camus describes a son's
growth from his mother outward towards the world as an organic process and as an abandonment. He owes his way of feeling things to a receding figure but it is he who is moving away.
This separation was to become aggravated in Camus' case because his mother had been poor and totally uneducated while
he himself, living in Paris, would enjoy international fame and
considerable wealth. We must also remember that if Camus ide-
alizes poverty in the *Carnets*, he also wrote *La Mort heureuse*,
never published in his lifetime, whose hero displays a love of
wealth at times crass and vulgar. It would be a long time before
Camus would courageously admit in *Le Premier homme*, his last,
unfinished novel, how ashamed he was of his poor family and
ashamed of his shame.[9] Sartre knew where to strike during their
quarrel when he wrote: "Il se peut que vous ayez été pauvre mais
vous ne l'êtes plus."[10]

9. Paul Viallaneix, *Le Premier Camus*, Suivi de *Ecrits de Jeunesse*, *Cahiers Albert
Camus*, 2 (Mayenne: Gallimard, 1973):23.
10. "Réponse à Albert Camus," *Situations*, 4 (Paris: Gallimard, 1964):93.

The "bad conscience" Camus describes goes far beyond the inevitable separation of mothers and sons, and *L'Etranger* examines that region where the inevitable is the result of human will and where the will is criminal.

L'Etranger replaces the diary's description of menaced continuity between mother and son with an abrupt break: "Aujourd'hui, maman est morte. Ou peut-être hier, je ne sais pas. J'ai reçu un télégramme de l'asile: 'Mère décédée. Enterrement demain. Sentiments distingués.' Cela ne veut rien dire. C'était peut-être hier" (TRN, 1127). This paragraph at first yields little more than the fact of death and an attempt to fix the precise time. The expression of sorrow we would reasonably expect from a son is not recorded. What arouses our curiosity is that Meursault concentrates more on the time of death than on the death itself. Such disproportion may well be the stylistic sign of a personal dilemma, and the following passages confirm our initial impression that more is involved than mere arithmetic:

L'asile est à deux kilomètres du village. J'ai fait le chemin à pied. J'ai voulu voir maman tout de suite. (TRN, 1128)

Il [le directeur] m'a dit: "Je suppose que vous voulez voir votre mère." Je me suis levé sans rien dire. (TRN, 1128)

"On l'a couverte mais je dois dévisser la bière pour que vous puissiez la voir." Il s'approchait de la bière quand je l'ai arrêté. Il m'a dit: "Vous ne voulez pas?" J'ai répondu: "Non." (TRN, 1129)

Meursault's desire to see his mother diminishes as their closeness increases. There is evidence in the first chapter that the fact of his mother's death has not really registered in his mind. The unequivocal affirmation of "aujourd' hui, maman est morte" is considerably modified by the evasive "ou peut-être hier." "Cela ne veut rien dire," Meursault adds, and a banal telegram becomes a cryptic message from a modern Sibyl. When the blunt evidence of the body is made available, however, Meursault recoils and avoids the confrontation. As a result, he allows a fact to fade into doubt. Remembering that he does not have a black tie Meursault comments: "Pour le moment, c'est un peu comme si maman n'était pas morte" (TRN, 1127). Reaching for a cigarette during the wake he observes: "J'ai hésité parce que je ne savais pas si je pouvais le faire devant maman" (TRN, 1131). This death is evidently unacceptable to Meursault. He wants to see his mother and he does not. She has just died but without visible proof she is not yet dead. That coffin in the middle of the room becomes a kind of theater in the round, a play celebrating an event all the more disturbing because one of the protagonists remains invisible. Meursault has denied the other mourners their right to see the dead body. He denies it to himself. Within the context of a banal, public vigil Meursault is celebrating his own private ritual.

Meursault's mother dies eventually, just as Meursault will, but not through any normal sequence of events and not of natural causes. The description of the burial reveals Meursault's purpose in maintaining at least the illusion of his mother's life:

Il y a eu encore l'église et les villageois sur les trottoirs, les géraniums rouges sur les tombes . . . la terre couleur de sang qui roulait sur la bière de maman, la chair blanche des racines qui s'y mêlaient, encore du monde, des voix, le village. (TRN, 1137)

The banal images of an oft-repeated routine are interrupted by a private vision of violence. Meursault's mother died of old age but the images of blood pouring down into the grave and the exposed white flesh shock us as would a brutal murder or primitive sacrifice. Later Meursault will explain to his lawyer: "Tous les êtres sains avaient plus ou moins souhaité la mort de ceux qu'ils aimaient" (TRN, 1172). He received the telegram, saw the coffin lowered into the grave, and it is at that moment that the images of violence invaded his mind. When Marie, who is shortly to become his mistress, asks on Saturday how long his mother has been dead, Meursault, who received the telegram on Thursday, answers: "Depuis hier" (TRN, 1139). Meursault places his mother's death on the day of the burial because that is the day he perceived it as violent. That violence existed only in his mind but his mind is where his mother was. Having no existence of her own, her son could destroy her with impunity. This act is transcribed into a journal that is less the image of reality than the outward form of his mind. Meursault's mother died "yesterday" and this time there is no more "perhaps."

A son may grow outward and away from his mother but only until her death. Youth may form the avant-garde but it is parents who die first, and the son's abandonment Camus speaks of in the *Carnets* is here reversed. Meursault sent his mother to a rest home and continued to occupy the same apartment. It is she who goes out but not into the world. The rest home is antechamber to the grave. Certainly in a Mediterranean society, not to care for one's mother is to abandon filial loyalty. In a larger sense, it denies the past. To forget, however, is to run the risk of being reminded by a telegram. Meursault's decision, therefore, to occupy the same apartment, like his decision not to view the dead body, allows him to thrust out the reality and retain the intangible image. On that level he enjoys unchallenged possession, in itself a demonstration of overwhelming love. After spending Sunday on his balcony observing what other people do, Meursault can conclude: "J'ai pensé que . . . maman était maintenant enterrée . . . et que, somme toute, il n'y avait rien de changé" (TRN, 1142). Has nothing really changed? There is a split in Meursault's character between what takes place outside, which is of no importance, and what takes place within, which is all important. Camus wants to idealize what we would normally consider a disintegrating personality. Meursault does not cry at the funeral. How could he if tears, acknowledging physical and emotional loss, proclaim our place in the biological and social processes of birth and death, the acquisition and loss of human ties? The acceptance of her natural death would have signified the acceptance of her abandonment. That kind of pain is unbearable to Meursault. Whether he kills her in his mind or introduces her as a character in his book, she becomes the image of her self, Meursault's creation. Nothing must precede or help define Meursault and his journal embodies this enterprise. The self is now consubstantial with a book, with words that are also the images of reality, and Meursault has his own beginning, middle, and end. While his style is impersonal, it serves a personal need. The question that remains is how this book, this life, will end.

After the funeral Meursault introduces several characters, more precisely several couples: himself and Marie, Raymond and his mistress, Salamano and his dog. Salamano brutalizes his dog until it finally escapes, and he later admits that he acquired the dog after his wife's death, a sort of substitute. Raymond, suspecting his mistress of infidelity, arranges for Meursault to write a letter enticing her back to the apartment. He plans to seduce her but to stop just at the point of orgasm and beat her. He goes through with his vengeance but her screams attract the police and she too escapes.

These men are linked to Meursault's life in several ways. All three are "neighbors," an arrangement that underscores their intimate relationship. Through the thin walls Meursault hears the woman's screams and Salamano's sobs over his loss. Within the story as Meursault composes it, each couple embodies a sordid and violent relationship. In each instance Meursault is a passive witness, just as he was at the funeral and afterwards on his balcony. To do nothing or simply to look on is to achieve the innocence of a bystander. That innocence is also in part aesthetic, not only because Meursault is an author and a book is silent speech, at one remove from reality, but because he wants to live his life with that same space between himself and others. As a man and an artist he remains outside the events he describes. Detachment includes observation but it shades into indifference when the event observed appears to have no relationship to the author describing. When Meursault, for example, finally confronts the Arab, brother of Raymond's mistress, he is genuinely surprised. Meursault does participate. But Meursault observing the burial or murdering that Arab is not the same thing as Salamano beating his dog, Raymond brutalizing his mistress, or even Caligula strangling Caesonia. They were all there. Meursault is not. Nor is it a question of intellectual superiority, man's ability, as we see in the heroes of Malraux, to keep something of himself in reserve, observing himself, weighing his actions, pronouncing judgments. Meursault does none of these things. By making Meursault indifferent, Camus solved the problem that confronted Caligula. Caligula knew what he was doing when he murdered and was always trying afterwards to justify his innocence with postgraduate logic. If he too, like Patrice Mersault, exercises oblivion it is always after the fact. Caligula's prompt remorse after the murder of Caesonia, however, revealed a fatal pause between the deed and the justification. Meursault abolishes that pause. He appears not to know what he is doing. He is or wants to be as much a stranger to himself as he is to others because he is or wants to be oblivious not after but during the act. Style and content meet in Meursault. His authorial strategy is to describe himself the way he conducts himself, mechanically, participating but uninvolved, a bystander, an innocent criminal.

This separation of body and mind, each one pursuing its separate goals, results in a double abstraction. Meursault's body is his sole link to the world. The gap within himself reproduces itself when Meursault must deal with other people. Meursault's affair with Marie shows no sign of degenerating into violence. Their relationship, however, when not enjoyed on the elementary level of sexual intercourse, is always out of balance when subjects other than sex come up. "Elle m'a demandé si je l'aimais. Je lui ai répondu que cela ne voulait rien dire" (TRN, 1151). Meursault's reply reproduces verbatim his own reaction to the telegram: "Cela ne veut rien dire." He does not accept the news of his mother's death and he does not accept the word *love*. Marie persists, however, and Meursault agrees to marry her. Marie assumes that love leads to marriage, a socially responsible union. She is asking Meursault to make some kind of commitment.

The murder of the Arab takes place during a Sunday outing at the beach. Meursault meets his two hosts, Masson who is "massif" and his wife who is "petite." They are reverse images of the family Meursault observed from his balcony: "Une mère énorme, en robe de soie marron, et le père, un petit homme assez frêle"[11] (TRN, 1140). Camus' purpose is to conjure up satirical images of domestic bliss. Meursault, however, also says things that sound strange coming from him: "Je lui ai dit combien je trouvais sa maison jolie. Il m'a appris qu'il y venait passer le samedi, le dimanche et tous ses jours de congé. 'Avec ma femme, on s'entend bien,' a-t-il ajouté. Justement sa femme riait avec

---

11. Roger Quilliot notes the same device in *La Peste*: "Présentation," *La Peste, Théâtre, Récits, Nouvelles d'Albert Camus* (Bruges: Gallimard, 1962), p. 1938.

Marie" (TRN, 1162). This Sunday, however, combines domesticity with murder. Meursault's passive participation in events is threatened by impending marriage. He will be involved with a community and he is already caught up in his own satire, his own ridicule. The situation of unwilling bachelor, banal enough, often comic, here comes into conflict with Meursault's self-centered nature. He is explicit: "Pour la première fois peut-être, j'ai pensé vraiment que j'allais me marier" (TRN, 1162). With this fact in mind, Meursault proceeds to make his choice and to kill the Arab.

At first, "choice" hardly seems an accurate description of Meursault's behavior or of the book's tone. The events leading to his confrontation with the Arab seem haphazard, a case of bad luck. We also note that, during their first walk on the beach, Raymond, Masson, and Meursault meet two Arabs and that Meursault does not join the fight. During a second walk, it is Raymond and Meursault who meet them. Raymond threatens to shoot but Meursault takes the gun away. The Arabs withdraw. At this crucial point Meursault cannot bring himself to return to the beachhouse: "Je suis resté devant la première marche, la tête retentissante de soleil, découragé devant l'effort qu'il fallait faire pour monter l'étage de bois et aborder encore les femmes" (TRN, 1166). He turns back and, seeking to escape the sun's heat, sees a boulder and walks toward its shade. There he meets the Arab. By both chance and a mathematical progression Meursault moves from the status of third party to that of protagonist, not without justice since it was he who wrote the letter that ultimately victimized the Arab's sister. Somnambulism and determinism, as in a dream, bring together in one man two of the essential facets of Camus' imperial vision, oblivion and grim purpose.

What, in effect, is Meursault's purpose? "Je pensais à la source fraîche derrière le rocher. J'avais envie de retrouver le murmure de son eau, envie de fuir le soleil, l'effort et les pleurs de femme, envie de retrouver l'ombre et son repos" (TRN, 1167). Women who weep, linking their inner feelings with external gestures and acknowledging pain and loss, are unbearable to Meursault who did not cry at his mother's funeral. Women and their tears (and their demands for marriage), the sun, and effort have at least one thing in common, public exposure and the inescapable conclusion that we are involved in human affairs. Meursault wants "l'ombre et son repos," stylistically a circumlocution for death, the absolutism of utter solitude. That rock, like a period, would end his life. Meursault's willingness to engage in sex but not marriage was already a kind of chastity. Here he is moving forward in order to withdraw. Meursault does not like to be asked questions and he does not like to explain. "L'innocent," Camus wrote in his notes, "est celui qui n'explique rien" (C, I, 90). When Marie asks "love" he answers "non-significance." As a character Meursault refuses to recognize the meanings of words, particularly words that reach his ears from the outside. As an author he can manipulate words either to make their meanings come only from him or to see to it they never acquire any meanings at all.

Meursault agreed to marry but events arranged themselves and/or were arranged by Meursault the protagonist and/or Meursault the author to put him within reach of a special kingdom: "Je voyais de loin la petite masse sombre du rocher entourée d'un halo aveuglant par la lumière et la poussière de mer" (TRN, 1167). The repose Meursault seeks is more than physical. This description has religious overtones, unifying darkness and light, the upper and lower worlds, a black sun. It is the repose from effort, from life itself, one that seems to promise an immobile sanctity. Existing on at least two levels, the glowing rock embodies a new self, a self not partially but this time totally removed from the human scene. What was for the swimmer in "Noces" a moment "cut out of the fabric of time" promises to become, for this swimmer, an eternity. The Arab, however, is there. Because of him or in spite of him, Meursault succeeds in escaping women, the sun, and effort. For the first time, however, there is deep stress and conflict in Meursault between his need to act unthinkingly and the effort he is making to reach that rock. He is in a predicament where effort is required to escape effort, where movement is required to achieve stasis. Up till now Meursault was able to write that letter, have Raymond deliver it, and then listen to the woman's screams. He could kill his mother in his mind because she was already dead. He could help set all these events in motion and remain the unmoved mover. The

Arab, however, is alive, vengeful, and there, and an explicit comparison is made between two events: "C'était le même soleil que le jour où j'avais enterré maman" (TRN, 1168). The comparison is possible because in both instances the victim is first disincarnated, deprived of physical reality. Consequently, Meursault's confrontation with the Arab is hallucinatory: "le front dans les ombres du rocher" (TRN, 1167); "je devinais son regard" (TRN, 1167); "Son image dansait devant mes yeux" (TRN, 1167); "A cause des ombres sur son visage, il avait l'air de rire" (TRN, 1168); "Mes yeux étaient aveuglés" (TRN, 1168). The Arab dissolves and this absence releases Meursault from moral responsibility. When the shot is fired, the entire emphasis is on the weapon, not the victim. Anxious "to flee" Meursault bends all of his efforts toward reproducing the scene of his mother's violent death, to dissolve the reality of the Arab, and replace him with an unsubstantial image. Without his mother Meursault could deny his past. The Arab now stands between him and his future. He killed his mother in his mind but he kills the Arab in the flesh and is arrested. Champigny describes the difference very well as "tuer moralement sa mère" and "tuer effectivement un Arabe."[12] The difference exists, however, in spite of Meursault's efforts. Having described the first shot as an accident, "the sun's fault" as he will explain at his trial, he proceeds to do what he set out to do, to kill a dead body: "J'ai tiré encore quatre fois sur un corps inerte où les balles s'enfonçaient sans qu'il y parût" (TRN, 1168).

Although his accusers are to become more concerned with the funeral than with the murder, Meursault's interrogation and trial necessarily begin with the Arab. Society generally seeks to integrate its moral and legal judgments with concrete evidence, but Meursault satirizes the proceedings effectively by being disinterested. His apathy stems in part from an extreme assumption that society is taking upon itself the responsibility of his life by investigating it, judging it, and condemning it. At the same time, Meursault's discovery that he may no longer be in control of his life and that society will kill him takes place within a jour-

12. *Sur un héros païen*, p. 133.

nal written in the first person and of which he is the sole author. Two systems of ethics and justice move on parallel tracks and never really meet.

Camus traces the entire courtroom scene over Malraux's depiction of Pierre Garine's trial in *Les Conquérants*. Justly accused of having arranged an illegal abortion, Garine too feels unnecessary. He describes the trial as a "spectacle irréel"[13] and a "comédie étrange."[14] These judgments, however, grow out of perceptions that differ radically from those of Meursault. Malraux wrote: "Tout montrait à Pierre le peu de relation entre les faits en cause et cette cérémonie."[15] The judicial system is then described as "absurde" because it disregards the facts and simplifies the complex, thereby rendering the events in life impossibly abstract. The prosecutor in *L'Etranger*, on the other hand, working back from the Arab's murder to the funeral, constructs an elaborate system of causes and effects and offers the jury a detailed *curriculum vitae*. He is eminently psychological and deals in motivation. Meursault, like Garine, also considers this construct artificial and abstract, not because it is bloodless but because it is in fact bloody. Garine objects to a loss of personality. Meursault, to his surprise, is told that he has one. Author of his journal, Meursault does not want to have a biography.

Meursault states that his imprisonment really begins after Marie's first and only visit. He does not want to see her and longs for his cell "plus calme et plus sombre" (TRN, 1178). We note that the same terms used to describe the rock now apply to the prison. When Marie leaves, his physical desires, his only real link to the world, leave with her. Having shed the opaque layers of social and biological responsibility, he is reduced to himself and has caught up with himself. Like the heroes of Stendhal, he is the tenant of a decor devoted to self-denial. Unlike Julien Sorel or Fabrice del Dongo, however, Meursault has no visible partner or companion.

The murder of the Arab does allow Meursault to gain access into the more intricate workings of his mind. In prison, his memory becomes active. He is more aware of his situation and

13. André Malraux, *Les Conquérants, Romans* (Bruges: Gallimard, 1947), p. 45.
14. Ibid.
15. Ibid.

his place in it. In my view, however, it would be incorrect to assume, as most critics do, that Meursault achieves greater authenticity, that his intellect or consciousness adds dimension to
his basically sensual nature. In prison, no such integration takes
place. His life, in fact, moves away from his body into his mind.
Before the murder, Meursault could disassociate the two and, as
a result, whatever the body did "signified" nothing. Marie and
the Arab, however, destroyed that arrangement because Meursault agreed to marry and then killed a man in the flesh. Left to
its own devices, the body can no longer be trusted. Meursault
will then reincorporate it into his mind where he intends to exercise total control. Such a movement, in its extremeness, is sterile, and Meursault's decapitation is the physical and tardy symbol of an operation he has already performed upon himself.
Meursault is a god but this time a god frightened by his body.
The athletic swimmer in "Noces à Tipasa" was sanctified in the
ocean because he swam alone. Meursault swam with Marie. Because the body, through its physical desires, runs the risk of
moral and social entanglements, Meursault will eventually condemn it.

Himself recently divorced when he began L'Etranger, Camus
wrote in the Carnets: "Renoncer à cette servitude qu'est l'atti-
rance féminine" (C, 1, 227). Attraction, marriage, and fidelity
become synonyms for bondage. Even prison, an approximation
of that self-contained and impenetrable rock Meursault sought
on the beach, must not last. It is prison plus capital punishment.
Meursault will cooperate with the condemnation because it
serves his plan to end his journal, his life, by himself. Robert
Champigny stresses this point: "La condamnation à mort l'a-
mène à considérer sa vie comme un tout. . . . Meursault vivait
(imparfait), maintenant il a vécu sa vie; il est encore vivant mais
ce qu'il pense avoir à vivre, c'est l'avoir vécu."[16] Once ended, a
life becomes a script. What we should add to Professor Champigny's perceptive remarks is that Meursault has always wanted
to live a life where nothing happened. That transcendance
which the rock promised, the prison will deliver. We can therefore understand Meursault's refusal to see the priest and his

16. *Sur un héros païen*, p. 167.

hysterical anger when he comes anyway. The priest affirms the supernatural continuity of a life that Meursault wishes to end. He speaks of God but Meursault has no intention of abandoning authorship of his own life, his journal. He alone will sponsor himself. There are no gods, or anyone else, before or after him. There is only *his* life.

Meursault discovers, however, that his body will not reject life and its entanglements so easily. It has too many involuntary muscles:

Ce qui me gênait un peu dans mon raisonnement, c'était ce bond terrible que je sentais en moi à la pensée de vingt ans de vie à venir. Mais je n'avais qu'à l'étouffer. (TRN, 1206)

Je me donnais . . . la permission d'aborder la deuxième hypothèse: j'étais gracié. L'ennuyeux, c'est qu'il fallait rendre moins fougueux cet élan du sang et du corps qui me piquait les yeux d'une joie insensée. Il fallait que je m'applique à réduire ce cri, à le raisonner. (TRN, 1206)

The body's sole remaining emotions are fear of death and love of life and Meursault will suppress both. He will succeed when he rejects any possibility of a reprieve, when he makes the separation between himself and society absolute: "Je venais de rejeter mon pourvoi et je pouvais sentir les ondes de mon sang circuler régulièrement en moi" (TRN, 1206). By rejecting his lawyer's appeal and guaranteeing his execution, by taking this extraordinary initiative, Meursault calms his body and makes his blood lie down. He realizes that the integration within himself required that everything exist in his mind and that whatever enters his mind must suffer disincarnation. While it is true that the mental processes are in fact once removed from concrete reality, Meursault would make unreality permanent.

In his journal Meursault describes events that happen to him. He cannot, however, record every moment of his life. Those same events, because they are selected and arranged, emanate from him. Narrating in the first person and unfettered by another point of view, Meursault tells us all he wants us to know. An apparently passive and indifferent man, therefore, aware of the factor of chance in everyday life, is in fact composing, out of this formless material, a coherent and cogently structured narrative. Behind the unfortunate, apparently unrelated and opaque events of a mother's funeral, an impending marriage, and a murder lies a lucid intelligence and a purpose. Meursault's journal embodies a fiction that is barely distinguishable from Meursault's life. Both are totalitarian because both seek absolute self-containment through mental indifference or the physical destruction of other lives.

Caligula's desire for "eternal solitude" required countless murders. He discovers, however, that he is only partially successful and disdains what he calls "cette solitude empoisonnée de présences" (TRN, 59). Those presences refer both to the images of those he killed and of those citizens who are still alive. Although he wishes otherwise, he cannot stop his body, vibrating under the impact of multiple murders, from sending messages to his brain. Meursault avoids such physical and violent confrontations to the point of describing his murder of the Arab as a bad dream. Both Caligula and Meursault discover that physical violence, like the mass assassinations, the beating of Sintès' mistress, and the murder of the Arab force the intervention of third parties and their moral inquiries. Henceforth Meursault is at attention. "Je veux être indifférent" (PC, 188). Camus announced before writing L'Etranger and we are hard put to decide which word is more important, "veux" or "indifférent." The terms, after all, are mutually exclusive. But it is precisely those two terms that help to explain the style of L'Etranger, a style suited to its hero who, until his imprisonment, is both willful and indifferent, present and absent. Caligula never faced this problem in the same way because he wanted to be indifferent after the crime. He wanted the pleasure of knowing what he was doing and then, like Patrice Mersault in La Mort heureuse, that of forgetting it. Camus was much more ambitious in L'Etranger. What had once been a horizontal sequence of events in time now had to be simultaneous, to be vertical. Whereas Caligula and Patrice Mersault could try to suppress the memory of what they did, how much worthier of a god not to have to suppress at all.

Meursault never experienced remorse because he never had

to. To this extent alone, Camus' experiment to see if a man, in order to transcend his humanity, could kill his mother without guilt is successful. Meursault, however, kills an image of his mother and the murder is more literary than literal. It is incomplete because it makes the transition from the mind directly into the pages of his journal. For these reasons, Meursault's trial is in fact absurd. The jury condemned an author and his book.

While Meursault does not express remorse, he does have a reunion with his mother in prison. She comes back to life through an aroused memory: "C'était d'ailleurs une idée de maman, et elle le répétait souvent, qu'on finissait par s'habituer à tout" (TRN, 1180). "Maman disait souvent qu'on n'est jamais tout à fait malheureux" (TRN, 1205). What she says never rises above the cliché, but in the context of death row these clichés are bits of evidence of the intimacy Meursault shared with his mother in their apartment. Because of Camus' calculated ambiguities it is a completely open question whether this intimacy is what Meursault always wanted but was afraid of as a free man, or whether he was truly deflected from his goal by the Arab's vengeance, that solitary rock occupying a point precisely midway between light and darkness, land and water, a part of the world and yet without feelings, an impenetrable symbol of the nonhuman.

His mother's exile and death may have freed Meursault of the human condition but they inspired his journal, his new life. Meursault knows this, which is why he spends so much time denying the evidence of the telegram. His new life begins with her death but her death must not be natural, that is to say an event that takes place beyond the sphere of absolute self-possession. If the telegram is false, and Meursault makes it false, then his journal did not begin *in medias res*. It would have its own "in the beginning," its year one. In the first entry of the *Carnets*, Camus already speaks of the separation between himself and his mother and, though only twenty-two, is making assessments and formulating tentative conclusions about his guilt.

In *L'Etranger* the distance between Meursault and his mother is greatest at the beginning. It is the distance between a son who will not cry and a mother invisible beneath the coffin's lid. In prison, Meursault is reduced to himself and invisible to a world that also has no intention of crying. Reiterating Caligula's "la haine autour de moi" Meursault, on the day of his execution, wants to be greeted "avec des cris de haine" (TRN, 1212). Since he has taken his dead mother's place, there is reason to assume that the equation is complete, and that the public's hatred of Meursault is equal to Meursault's hatred of his mother. Camus knows something that Meursault only suspects. Through Meursault and against Meursault, Camus examines to what extent a mother can be alienated from her son's life all the while occupying its very center. He described this attraction and opposition in *L'Envers et l'endroit* as "l'image désespérante et tendre d'une solitude à deux" (E, 27). Apparently, the blood that pours down on the coffin is as much Meursault's as it is his mother's. When Camus, to free himself, announced his decision to be indifferent, he also knew how indifferent his mother was, the mother who never told her son she loved him, "l'indifférence de cette mère étrange" (E, 26). Meursault discovers too late that his mother's death embodied, not liberation, but his own future, not only his condemnation but that sonhood he felt deeply and also wanted to deny. Camus' mother was illiterate and virtually a mute. Composed of silent words, his book, Meursault's journal, is both for her and against her.

"Si près de la mort, maman devait s'y sentir libérée et prête à tout revivre. . . . Et moi aussi, je me suis senti prêt à tout revivre" (TRN, 1211). "Me too," Meursault says, like a child who, though in revolt, ends up following in his mother's footsteps. Both her life and her death preceded his, however desperately he wanted to break that cycle.

Meursault reads a story of how a mother killed her son who had returned home after many years and refused to identify himself. Having read the story "des milliers de fois" (TRN, 1182), he calls it both "invraisemblable" and "naturelle" (TRN, 1182). Likewise in *Le Malentendu*, a play based on that story, a mother kills her son and, after discovering his identity, kills herself. It then becomes impossible to say, as in *L'Etranger*, who killed whom. Germaine Brée makes it clear that, in *Le Malentendu*, "the victim has written a script of his own."[17] Martha, the most intelligent character in the play, explains the purpose of

17. *Camus*, p. 155.

that script with blunt, incestuous imagery: "Ma mère a rejoint son fils. Le flot commence à les ronger. On les découvrira bientôt et ils se retrouveront dans la même terre. . . . Je les laisse à leur tendresse retrouvée, à leurs caresses obscures" (TRN, 176). The same insights, within limits, may well be applied to Meursault's journal. Allowing for his specialized, psychoanalytic vocabulary, Alain Costes points up the major difference between the two texts: "Ce qui était latent-refoulé-dans *L'Etranger* est devenu manifeste dans *Le Malentendu*."[18]

Meursault "reads" about this murder and claims that it is and is not applicable to his own life and death. Camus and the reader know, however, that Meursault exiled his mother and killed her in his mind. She returns in the form of a Muse and as a living memory, that human content Meursault wanted to abolish through impersonal style. Mother to the end, her death inspired a book where her son, Meursault, faithful to the name which, after all, she gave him, records his dutiful "leap into death."

18. *Albert Camus ou la parole manquante*, pp. 136–37.

2 / Commitment and Strategies for Innocence

AFTER *L'Etranger* and after the curtain came down in *Le Malentendu*, Camus had gone as far as he could in imagining a murder and suicide pact between a mother and son. He had come to a dead end in the completely literal sense of that phrase.

That there was a pact at all must have been both surprising and reassuring to Camus, surprising because the main thrust of *La Mort heureuse*, *Caligula*, *L'Etranger*, and *Le Malentendu* is the free exercise of absolute self-sufficiency, reassuring because the activist journalist and author of *L'Envers et l'endroit* rediscovered human ties in the process of destroying them.

In *Le Mythe de Sisyphe*, Camus argues against suicide and, to that extent, against the major works he had already produced. Meursault, for example, was indifferent to human life and decided to die rather than show interest, to preserve himself from any invasion of his absolute privacy. Whereas his intellect succeeded in dominating his body and its fears of death, we now read: "Le jugement du corps vaut bien celui de l'esprit et le corps recule devant l'anéantissement. Nous prenons l'habitude de vivre avant d'acquérir celle de penser" (E, 102). The movement back to the body coincides with a reaffirmation of life. Camus suggests that insofar as the mind is capable of removing itself from the body and from concrete reality in general, it is allied with death, with total abstraction, the ultimate denial of the flesh it predeceases. Camus' critique of Heidegger and Kierkegaard is directed not only against their particular philosophies but, in large part, against pure intellection itself. Of the heroes proposed for our admiration in *Le Mythe de Sisyphe*, the actor, the artist, the conqueror, and Don Juan, none claim or merit the title of intellectual. If anything, Meursault deserves it more than they. The sole purpose of Camus' new heroes is to live life passionately. Up to a certain point, *Le Mythe* is a corrective to the indifference to life Camus had once deemed appropriate for his characters and for his own personal conduct

The narrator of *Le Mythe de Sisyphe* describes the crisis of a man who has reached thirty years of age, the traditional turning point in life's journey: "Il se situe par rapport au temps. Il y prend sa place. Il reconnaît qu'il est à un certain moment d'une courbe qu'il confesse devoir parcourir. Il appartient au temps et, à cette horreur qui le saisit, il y reconnaît son pire ennemi. . . . Cette révolte de la chair, c'est l'absurde" (E, 107). Since Camus was twenty-seven when he wrote these lines, the crisis, three years early, is his. He is afraid of death but less willing to suppress that fear. While it is true that Meursault's life was taken from him, it was a life he was willing to give. He gained a superior, independent existence through his journal, a *vita nuova* he alone controlled. Through the medium of the text he would end his recorded life at approximately the same moment society ended the real one. Now Camus is not so sure. He would now prefer to "take his place" in time rather than kill it.[1] The awareness of time is particularly acute because thirty is still a young age, and because youth, more in the body than in the mind,

---

1. The text, too, is doomed: "Savoir que sa création n'a pas d'avenir, voir son oeuvre détruite en un jour en étant conscient que, profondément, cela n'a pas

revolts against what the mind knows to be true. In a sense *L'Etranger* was written by a young man who had been unexpectedly stricken with tuberculosis, an athlete betrayed by his body, *Le Mythe de Sisyphe* by an older man who survived a mortal disease only to be confounded by his mortality. The absurd, therefore, not only mobilizes a revolt, but a revolt that would make no sense unless death really existed. Since revolt becomes the sole catalyst through which a man progresses from indifference, or else from a lethargic confidence in his eternal life, into a state of lucidity, then he must remain faithful not only to his revolt but to the knowledge of death that inspired it. Meursault calmed his body but here the body, to maintain its revolt, must keep the mind fully alert. The only objective truth Camus can formulate, his mortality, is the very truth he finds both intolerable and necessary if he is to be truly alive: "Si je juge qu'une chose est vraie, je dois la préserver. . . . La première et, au fond, la seule condition de mes recherches, c'est de préserver cela même qui m'écrase (E, 121). The knowledge of death, by this declension, becomes a vital stimulus. Camus had written: "Tout commence par la conscience et rien ne vaut que par elle" (E, 107). Whatever threatens to dim that glare is rejected. It is a question of integrating, not opposing, mind and body, the knowledge of death and the appetite for life. Suicide and doctrines of immortality, therefore, are gathered by Camus under the general, derisive heading of evasions or "sauts" because, in the confrontation between life and death, they each suppress one of its crucial terms, resulting in physical annihilation or passivity.

Camus, however, is not satisfied to know. He must know once and for all. Such permanence can only be guaranteed by personal adhesion. As a result, knowledge overlaps into physical activity and possession. Whatever a priori truths may exist will remain abstract unless incarnated in a specific personality and eventually indistinguishable from it. If death is terrifying it also offers the profound satisfaction of being a fact. The impulse to

---

plus d'importance que de bâtir pour des siècles, c'est la sagesse difficile que la pensée absurde autorise" (E, 189–90). Earlier in the essay Camus had written: "Du point de vue de Sirius, les oeuvres de Goethe dans dix mille ans seront en poussière et son nom oublié" (E, 158).

know absolutely, therefore, has its source as much in the human desire to possess as in the human mind to know:

> Comprendre c'est avant tout unifier. Le désir profond de l'esprit . . . rejoint le sentiment inconscient de l'homme devant son univers: il est exigence de familiarité, appétit de clarté. Comprendre le monde pour un homme, c'est le réduire à l'humain, le marquer de son sceau. . . . Cette nostalgie d'unité, cet appétit d'absolu illustrent le mouvement essentiel du drame humain. (E, 110)

Whether the self expands to fill the world or appropriates it into its own constellation, the goal is to equate knowledge with self-possession. A group of abstract and unrelated truths will be caught up and redesigned once they have passed through the intricate networks of the self. One can therefore understand why Camus' critique of various philosophies often turns into commentary on the philosopher. They are consubstantial. He applies the same methods to himself when he states: "L'idée d'un art détaché de son créateur n'est pas seulement démodée. Elle est fausse" (E, 175). Such a point of view is romantic because it demands that an aesthetic or philosophical system be lived, incarnated in the person of the artist or philosopher and demonstrated in his conduct. If Camus often looks to Malraux and Montherlant for guidance, it is because they, too, are the athletes of philosophy.

What Camus records bitterly in Le Mythe de Sisyphe, however, is his failure to achieve such a synthesis. He laments his inability to know (possess) either himself or the world: "Si j'essaie de saisir ce moi dont je m'assure, si j'essaie de le définir et de le résumer, il n'est plus qu'une eau qui coule entre mes doigts" (E, 111); "Comment nierais-je ce monde dont j'éprouve la puissance et les forces? Pourtant toute la science de cette terre ne me donnera rien qui puisse m'assurer que ce monde est à moi" (E, 111). Meursault had no such ambitions to the sole extent that he was satisfied with negative definitions of himself. Camus in his essay strives for something positive and ends up caught in a "tournoiement vertigineux" (E, 110). To understand the world is to mark it with one's seal but Camus discovers in death an even greater artist ready to mark him with extinction.

The solution Camus proposes is to build his life around the one and only notion, his death, of which he is certain. This decision places him in a world perhaps best described as death's dominion, the world of flux, incessant change, politics, and history. Here an artist-emperor, an indifferent son, a swimmer without a memory, for the time being, have no place.

While *Le Mythe* is not, strictly speaking, a political or historical treatise, its perspective opens up to include certain political and historical issues. When Camus finished the first part in 1940, he had left Algeria as a persona non grata,[2] and Germany had invaded France; when he completed the manuscript a year later, he had joined the Resistance. In 1939, at about the time war had been declared, Camus expressed this private opinion:

Juger un événement est impossible et immoral si c'est du dehors. C'est au sein de cet absurde malheur qu'on conserve le droit de le mépriser. . . . Vouloir . . . planer et se séparer de son milieu, c'est faire l'épreuve la plus dérisoire des libertés. Voilà pourquoi il fallait que j'essaie de servir. Et si l'on ne veut pas de moi, il faut que j'accepte la position du civil dédaigné. Dans les deux cas, mon jugement peut demeurer absolu et mon dégoût sans réserves. (C, 1, 172–73)

Camus is anxious not to become, in his own mind and for others, a spokesman for ivory towers. Such fears were of course groundless in view of his activities as a journalist and member of the Communist party. Nevertheless, many of his articles on the impending war did have a strong pacifist slant[3] and nonalign-

2. Because of the war, Camus' newspaper articles in *Alger républicain* and *Soir républicain*, together with those of his friend and editor Pascal Pia, were systematically censured. Roger Quilliot summarizes the consequences: "Camus et Pia faisaient . . . paraître un article préalablement censuré et adressaient aux censeurs une lettre vigoureuse qui leur valait un blâme. Ensuite de quoi, le 10 janvier 1940, le *Soir républicain* était suspendu par décision du gouverneur général. Le conseil d'administration, ou ce qui en tenait lieu, désireux d'obtenir l'autorisation de reparaître, accusait Camus de sabotage. . . . Pascal Pia regagnait Paris en février 1940, et devenait secrétaire de rédaction à *Paris-Soir*, *l'Auto* et *la Lumière*. Il présentait . . . la candidature d'Albert Camus pour un poste de secrétaire de rédaction. Celui-ci le rejoignait en mars 1940. Une autre période de sa vie commençait" (E, 1367).

3. Quilliot points out that Camus was particularly impressed by Jean Giono's

ment could have been interpreted in just such a light. His wish to serve, expressed most forcefully in this passage from the *Carnets*, is evident as well in *Le Mythe de Sisyphe* and partially responsible for its impact on the reader. We note, however, that commitment is not viewed as sacrificial or even as a risk a person takes for certain political goals. Camus considers it a method to preserve the integrity of private judgment, in particular scorn. There is no question of psychological or political modifications operating within an individual in response to events. If we were to define the posture Camus assumes towards history, we would call it aristocratic. In the chapter entitled "La Conquête," he writes: "Je ne fais tant de cas de l'individu que parce qu'il m'apparaît dérisoire et humilié. . . . J'ai du goût pour les causes perdues" (E, 165). He adds a little further on: "C'est le monde qui le broie et c'est moi qui le libère" (E, 165–66). This posture owes much to the series of essays the disdainful Montherlant published in 1935 under the significant title: *Service Inutile*.[4] Camus, like his predecessor, feels both committed and uninvolved, the latter sentiment based on the conviction that he is fighting someone else's war. Careful to define exactly what he owes to the survival of society, Camus is signalling an important turning point in his life. He will commit himself to a global crisis. His vocabulary acquires such terms as "mon temps," "l'histoire," "action," and "fraternité." And when, early in the book, Camus declares: "Pour toujours, je serai étranger à moi-même" (E, 111), he is not only giving shape to a tragic vision, but offering himself as well, under the pressure of political turmoil, the cue for unfettered action, for the full, uncensored release of energies whose course he would chart later. In the meantime, impatient with study or reflection (The mind can know nothing except its certain death.), he expresses contempt for no less a figure than Socrates: "Le 'connais-toi toi-même' de Socrate a autant de valeur que le 'sois vertueux' de nos confessionnaux. . . . Ce sont des jeux stériles sur de grands sujets" (E, 111).

Lettre aux paysans sur la pauvreté et la paix, a pacifist appeal published early in 1939, although he did not accept all of Giono's premises concerning nonviolence (E, 1371).

4. *Essais* (Bruges: Gallimard, 1965), pp. 571–735.

Meursault's indifference which cut him off from the examination of his own life and of other people has been modified to the extent that Camus has mobilized his energies toward the specific goals of service and "liberation." Self-analysis, however, remains a "sterile game," and commitment coexists with that other respectful distance separating the victims from their liberator. *Le Mythe de Sisyphe*, therefore, appears, at first glance, to be an apology for a systematic, more respectable, and more knowing superficiality.

In contrast, the life that Camus once had led and then described in the lyrical essay "Noces à Tipasa" derived its fulfillment from the physical and private apprehension of Nature. His man-god enjoyed the total possession of the sea and the sky. In *Le Mythe*, however, "world" more and more comes to mean "society." A passage from the *Carnets* offers an opportunity to evaluate this change of direction: "Jeune, on adhère mieux à un paysage qu'à un homme. C'est que les premiers se laissent interpréter" (C, 1, 48). Interpretation offers the observer, particularly if he is young, a gratifying demonstration of his imaginative powers which are based, if we are reading "se laissent" correctly, on the consent or passivity of Nature. Camus takes quite a different position in *Le Mythe*. Nature is now "épais," a stone "irréductible." It is not knowable and it is closed to any future probes. Ignorance is not only attributable, as we have seen, to the inability of the mind to discover permanent truths (other than death) but also to the transformation of Nature from passive accomplice to active opponent:

Voici l'étrangeté: s'apercevoir . . . avec quelle intensité . . . un paysage peut nous nier. . . . Ces collines, la douceur du ciel, ces dessins d'arbres, voici qu'à la minute même, ils perdent le sens illusoire dont nous les revêtions, désormais plus lointains qu'un paradis perdu. L'hostilité primitive du monde, à travers les millénaires, remonte vers nous. (E, 107–8)

What had once been knowledge is now reevaluated as an illusory configuration of the mind. Possession sours into a lost paradise. The illusion, furthermore, is double-edged. The meanings Camus thought he discovered in Nature were thrust upon Nature; what had been the sign and proof of the self's powers of observation were in fact the intolerable evidence of its weakness. When Camus adds: "Le monde nous échappe puisqu'il redevient lui-même" (E, 108), he realizes that the possession of landscapes was possible because the lyricist saw Nature in terms of images, in other words in terms of his own desires. Contemplation translated itself into assimilation. The world that "becomes itself" resists that process because the self, singing solo, is able to affirm itself only at the expense of someone or something else's anonymity. To know is to annihilate the thing known. Total possession requires it. Investing the external object with its own desire for knowledge, the self renders it transparent, emptied of content. Objectively, therefore, a man cannot simultaneously comprehend the world and preserve it. If he cannot preserve it, he loses his base of power. For compensation he turns to the social problems he knows he can solve pragmatically. The question then immediately arises whether the self's desire for unity, or permanence, can be satisfied in this way, whether the human community will be as receptive or as hostile to a liberator's ambitions.

Camus, for example, describes his sense of separation from Nature as a "divorce," the antonym of unity, and he does so enough times to allow us to speak of an obsession.[5] In so doing, he is constructing (or reconstructing) a specific biography. He writes: "La pensée d'un homme est avant tout sa nostalgie" (E, 134). That nostalgia corresponds to a man's brief union with the world. Camus, however, is not sure whether the separation of man and Nature goes back to the beginning of time, his intimacy little more than a spun illusion, or whether that unity did once exist but now, in his own words, a paradise lost. Is he a citizen or

---

5. Examples include: "Dans un univers soudain privé d'illusions et de lumières, l'homme se sent un étranger. . . . Ce divorce entre l'homme et sa vie, l'acteur et son décor, c'est proprement le sentiment de l'absurdité" (E, 101); "L'absurde est essentiellement un divorce. Il n'est ni dans l'un ni dans l'autre des éléments comparés. Il naît de leur confrontation" (E, 120); "Tout ce qui détruit, escamote, ou subtilise ces exigences (et en premier lieu le consentement qui détruit le divorce) ruine l'absurde" (E, 121); "L'homme intègre l'absurde et dans cette communion fait disparaître son caractère essentiel qui est opposition, déchirement et divorce" (E, 124).

a deposed king? He describes that paradise as a "monde familier" literally, as a reference to a son's relationship with his mother, his first apprehension of reality. He speaks of an "exigence de familiarité" (E, 110). He describes "le bonheur" (unity) and "l'absurde" (divorce) as "deux fils de la même terre" (E, 197). The metaphor of divorce, therefore, functions as a point of convergence for contradictory feelings: firstly, because the term describes not only a relationship with the world but a son's relationship with his mother; and secondly, because the term itself, already inappropriate in the dictionary sense, becomes more inappropriate still when Camus tells us that divorce is not, as we would normally expect, a parting of the ways, but a perpetual and unrelieved confrontation:

Ce monde . . . n'est pas raisonnable. . . . Mais ce qui est absurde, c'est la confrontation de cet irrationnel et de ce désir éperdu de clarté dont l'appel résonne au plus profond de l'homme. L'absurde dépend autant de l'homme que du monde. Il est pour le moment leur seul lien. Il les scelle l'un à l'autre comme la haine seule peut river les êtres. (E, 113)

Cet état de l'absurde, il s'agit d'y vivre. Je sais sur quoi il est fondé, cet esprit et ce monde arcboutés l'un contre l'autre sans pouvoir s'embrasser. (E, 128)

The resonance we normally expect from the language of love here derives from the language of hate, and we realize that confrontation and hatred are offered to us as the next best thing to communion. They are not presented as an antithesis to love but as an approximation, a state of the mind and heart one step removed from an ideal of bliss and its nostalgia. The importance of hate is not that it contradicts love but that in Camus' view, it keeps us, like love but for want of love, in physical contact. The difference, and it is a major difference, is that two will never become one, and that the man-god has met resistance. Le Mythe de Sisyphe examines Nature's hostility, the self's emotional recoil, and its compensation through political commitment.

The transition from unity to divorce, however, is not altogether a transition from positive to negative. Enough evidence indicates the opposite may also be true. If Camus meets resistance in Nature, he himself offers resistance to his mother. Because Nature is personified by Camus, it is difficult to determine whether Nature and mother are or are not equivalent terms to be used interchangeably. Is Camus ambivalent towards the same reality or is he examining opposite feelings toward two distinct realities? While they may share certain common features, as in the cliché "Mother Earth," the following passage which describes both a mother's and a wife's love indicates that Camus is making a distinction:

> Ceux qu'un grand amour détourne de toute vie personnelle s'enrichissent peut-être, mais appauvrissent à coup sûr ceux que leur amour a choisis. Une mère, une femme passionnée, ont nécessairement le coeur sec, car il est détourné du monde. Un seul sentiment, un seul être, un seul visage, mais tout est dévoré. (E, 154–55)

Oneness is not in Camus but in the loving, omnipotent, wholly "other"; it is the beloved, or Camus, who is here rendered anonymous, the nightmare version of a once cherished unity. Hatred may still tie us to each other but our separate wills and identities are preserved. The mother Camus describes here, however, does not resemble the passive and indifferent mother in *L'Envers et l'endroit*. His description organizes itself instead around what he either thinks or hopes may have been his mother's love for him, so absolute as to justify the verb "dévorer." This portrait may or may not be accurate but Camus gets the results he wants. The public, often incoherent but freer lives we lead in a society will, in contrast to the "grand amour," appear healthy. When Camus announces his commitment in *Le Mythe de Sisyphe*, he proclaims it superficial by comparison with the communion with Nature;[6] at the same time he proclaims it salutory, an escape from possessive love and the anonymity that attends it. Camus is working out of and against nostalgia just as, in the

6. In 1947, Camus wrote in his notebooks: "J'ai relu tous ces cahiers—depuis le premier. Ce qui m'a sauté aux yeux: les paysages disparaissent peu à peu. Le cancer moderne me ronge moi aussi" (C, 2, 206). In 1945, referring to Hegel's equation of the modern city and self-awareness, Camus had added: "C'est le temps des grandes villes. On a amputé le monde d'une partie de sa vérité, de ce qui fait sa permanence et son équilibre: la nature, la mer, etc." (C, 2, 160).

opening entry of the *Carnets*, a son proceeded out of and against his mother.

To this extent, the energies in *Le Mythe* are not directed vertically downward as they are in *Noces, Caligula*, or *L'Etranger*, that is to say towards total self-possession. Its perspective is becoming horizontal, historically oriented, with more emphasis on multiple human relationships, out of necessity since Nature resists our manipulation, out of choice since Camus himself does not want to be annulled by someone else's love. When Camus defines the absurd as "la raison lucide qui constate ses limites" (E, 134) and genius as "l'intelligence qui connaît ses frontières" (E, 152), both Nature and self are liberated from any imperial enterprise, from that stasis Meursault enjoyed in prison, a divine state where everything exists in the mind. Thus Nature and man, mother and son, familiar once, now strangers, give way in *Le Mythe de Sisyphe* to a consideration of social organizations.

Camus, however, is not merely shifting the burden of lyricism from Nature onto a set of social realities. He demonstrates the meaninglessness of the general world and applies the nihilism of absurd "insignificance" with equal force to its human part. Strangeness and separatedness also pervade our dealings with others. Camus also calls our attention to a significant difference, one that justifies his decision to renew human ties:

Il est probablement vrai qu'un homme nous demeure à jamais inconnu et qu'il y a toujours en lui quelque chose d'irréductible qui nous échappe. Mais *pratiquement*, je connais les hommes et je les reconnais à leur conduite, à l'ensemble de leurs actes, aux conséquences que leur passage suscite dans la vie. (E, 105)

Camus himself underlines the "practicality" of his enterprise. The private, speculative depths evident in *Noces, Caligula*, and *L'Etranger* give way in life, in prose as it were, to a view wide enough to place in the foreground our physical gestures and conduct, our visible and public identities. In short, we know each other to the extent that we see each other act. This politics of the body and of the external man, not unlike Sartre's "situations," accounts for such synonyms as "histoire" and "action." They have in common verifiable behavior subject to external influence and interpretation and consequently to perpetual adjustment. Camus is now extraordinarily aware of stepping out of one way of life into another: "Conscient que je ne puis me séparer de mon temps, j'ai décidé de faire corps avec lui. . . . Entre l'histoire et l'éternel, j'ai choisi l'histoire parce que j'aime les certitudes. . . . Il vient toujours un temps où il faut choisir entre la contemplation et l'action. Cela s'appelle devenir un homme" (E, 165). The youth who preferred landscapes saturated with his own personality and who had painful memories of an overwhelming love is now an adult, and World War II, whether it spared him or killed him, would confirm his manhood and his commitment to the human community.

The transition in *Le Mythe de Sisyphe* from contemplation to action, to a keener sense of community, would suggest a Camus once more engaged in a populated and relativistic world, a world of pragmatic issues, similar to the ones he dealt with as a journalist in Algeria, except international in scale. It suggests that the quest for absolute self-absorption, characteristic of the imperial vision, is absent. This quest, however, is still very much present and, as a result, *Le Mythe de Sisyphe* is rich in contradictions.

Whenever Camus stresses the participatory nature of the self, as he does in *Noces* and *Le Mythe*, he exalts the body, theater of the physical. Death, consequently, is revealed in the very locus of vitality. The body adjusts its rhythm to the rhythm of change. At the same time, the man in action reveals something of his inner identity.

One of the models Camus proposes for the ideal absurd man, however, is the actor. An actor maintains the equilibrium that Camus seeks between the grim seriousness of life and surface "play" which, like art, may at times encompass it. Acting, however, is not viewed solely as a profession, one in which Camus himself excelled. It becomes a model for our relationship with others and defines what Camus means by participation:

Il est certain qu'apparemment, pour avoir vu cent fois le même acteur, je ne l'en connaîtrai personnellement pas mieux. Pourtant si je fais la somme des héros qu'il a incarnés et si je dis que je le connais un peu plus au centième personnage recensé, on sent qu'il y aura là une part de

vérité. Car ce paradoxe apparent est aussi un apologue. Il a une mora-
lité. Elle enseigne qu'un homme se définit aussi bien par ses comédies
que par ses élans sincères. Il en est aussi . . . des sentiments, inac-
cessibles dans le coeur, mais partiellement trahis par les actes qu'ils
animent. . . . Je définis une méthode . . . mais cette méthode est d'analyse et non de connaissance. . . . La méthode définie ici confesse le sentiment que toute vraie connaissance est impossible. Seules les appa-
rences peuvent se dénombrer et le climat se faire sentir. (E, 105–6)

The actor interests Camus because he too is an athlete. He is on
display in society and, whether he lies or speaks the truth, he is
partially identifying himself. He allows for the interpretation of
his actions and, consequently, to some form of social assimilation. Meursault, too, was "interpreted," but he remained a total
stranger to the efforts of a society to identify him. Stepping back
into society, Camus envisions himself as an actor willing to be observed, if not judged.

But it is the role, not the man, that is really exposed. His "morality" is not, as we would normally expect, based on his rapport
with others, on participation, but rather on an exclusive relationship with himself, the sequence he alone develops between
what he did and what he is now doing, the series of heroes he
incarnates. An actor on stage interprets the intentions of an author. An actor in society has his self-created identity. He is a fiction willing to link up with reality but on a parallel track and
without any real loss of prestige. In 1938, Camus defended Malraux against charges, coming from the political left, of "role-
playing":

C'est une mode aujourd'hui de condamner le romantisme révolutionnaire. Mais rien n'est plus difficile que de séparer, dans un homme,
la comédie qu'il se joue et l'instinct profond qui dicte ses actes. Il est
courant, par example, de dénoncer l'attitude romantique d'un écrivain
comme Malraux. . . . La question . . . est . . . de savoir s'il risque sa vie
tous les jours. . . . Ceci demeure notre seul critérium vérifiable.

Il y a dans tout héroïsme un peu de littérature. Et à force de répudier
le romantisme révolutionnaire, il faut craindre de divorcer avec la Révolution elle-même. (E, 1395–96)

Several years later Camus adopts a similar posture not for the Revolution but for the liberation of Europe against Nazism. Imitating Malraux, he will risk his life to preserve it from unnecessary scrutiny. The posture is heroic and heroism implies a style of life, a controlled life. An international crisis prompted Camus to, in his own words, "espouse his time." By the same token crises of such global dimensions placed Camus outside of time. The paradox in *Le Mythe* is that the meaninglessness of life makes life worth living. The political hyphen connecting these two opposing views was the fact of war. Mortality renders human initiative meaningless, absurd. At the same time, working *in extremis* robs time and our everyday gestures of their insufferable banality and endows them both with an heroic halo.

Speaking of men committed to action Camus writes: "Il n'y a qu'un seul luxe pour eux et c'est celui des relations humaines" (E, 167). "Luxe" takes human relationships outside of everyday contacts and their clichés and places them in a context of crisis. Because of war, it refers to menaced relationships. War, in turn, conscripts a small population of heroes who will liberate the oppressed. Camus speaks of fraternity but he means an elite. His description of the new brotherhood is Cornelian in its rhetorical and heroic emphases: "Visages tendus, fraternité menacée, amitié si forte et si pudique des hommes entre eux" (E, 167). Such intensity dissolves ordinary time divided into past, present, and future and puts in its place what Camus considers the ideal of the absurd man: "Le présent et la succession des présents devant une âme sans cesse consciente" (E, 145). "Succession" and "present moments" are as close as Camus can come to timelessness without altogether abandoning reality and its movement. Since all life ends in permanent death Camus rejects hope and with it the future. Since we are divorced from our former paradise, or hell, the past too is abolished. That lucidity and that consciousness, the moral foundations of the absurd man and his only justification for living, encompass time and all that time brings. As a result, nothing happens *to* him. Everything happens *in* him.

Le Mythe de Sisyphe, therefore, is more than a call to commitment. Having written *L'Etranger* and created Meursault who refused to go to Paris to advance his career, Camus is now telling us he is ambitious and made of sterner stuff. He does not have enough scorn for "cette éternité dérisoire qu'on appelle postérité" (E, 149); and he informs us that "de toutes les gloires, la moins trompeuse est celle qui se vit" (E, 158).

Camus, therefore, has not, for all that, abandoned indifference. The fact of death, once it has truly registered, allows the happy few to view life from the perspective of eternity and, as a result, makes indifference the only possible moral stance, our "noblesse profonde" (E, 158). Unlike Meursault's, however, this indifference is not suicidal. It does not outrun death. Indifference is our ultimate condemnation always present in our minds, and the condemned man, Camus tells us, is the opposite of the suicide (E, 138–39). More important for the purpose of this study, indifference guarantees the private integrity of a man who is politically committed. He makes moves toward us but we barely know him. What Camus is writing is a personal tract on heroism.

The hero, in espousing his time, is not espousing historical time but a cataclysm in history. His ultimate enemy is everyday life. Achilles, the heroic prototype, chose a short, glorious life over a long, obscure one and nothing has changed since Homer had him make that decision. Camus' hero must live in the present because only then can he control his life. "Le vrai problème," Camus wrote in 1942, "est . . . l'unité psychologique" (C, 2, 10). Unity achieved, a person becomes a personage. Camus is anxious to communicate both his belief in and fundamental distrust of experience. War, because it is extraordinary, allows for that temporary synthesis between psychological unity and the unforeseeable accidents of involvement, a life lived according to a prearranged scheme. He may be killed but he will die suddenly and completely, not in minuscule portions. That unity, however, is always threatened by the participatory nature of the self in a world where, according to Camus, "la dispersion est la règle" (Ibid). When the swimmer entered the ocean nude, he had total confidence in the cooperation of Nature: "La mer: je ne m'y perdais pas, je m'y retrouvais" (C, 2, 10). Society is less passive. Dispersion represents the fragmentation of the self responding to multiple commitments, as in everyday life. Camus' actor is willing to incarnate a series of personages in a sequence of his own devising. He would not tolerate multiple roles performed simultaneously. Such a situation could never place his entire identity solely within the precincts of his own self. Even as late as 1944 when, halfway through *La Peste*, Camus was seriously reevaluating the hero, he wrote in his diary: "Dégoût profond de toute société. Tentation de fuir et d'accepter la décadence de son époque. La solitude me rend heureux. Mais sentiment aussi que la décadence commence à partir du moment où l'on accepte. Et on reste. . . . Mais dégoût, dégoût nauséeux de cet éparpillement dans les autres" (C, 2, 135). These remarks catch up many of the feelings expressed in *Le Mythe de Sisyphe*: the uneasy alliance between political responsibility and fundamental indifference, between participation and the fear of losing one's identity. The hero's problem of psychological unity is compounded by the fact of having had a past, a pre-heroic existence: "L'obstacle, c'est la vie passée (profession, mariage, opinions passées, etc.), ce qui est déjà arrivé" (C, 2, 20). Such a past represents a threat to any attempt to project a new self-image because it constitutes facts. The past makes us psychological. Consequently, it is not only a question in *Le Mythe* of proclaiming a man's freedom, but of insisting on his freedom "from." A source of power needed to destroy biography and to replace it with freedom and fiction must have its locus somewhere in the human organism and Camus puts in the will. The actor, like the hero dedicated to appearance, incarnates that will: "Il illustre . . . cette vérité si féconde qu'il n'y a pas de frontière entre ce qu'un homme veut être et ce qu'il est. A quel point le paraître fait l'être, c'est ce qu'il démontre, toujours occupé de mieux figurer. Car c'est son art, cela, de feindre absolument" (E, 159–60). If the mind has its limits volition has none. Camus stated unequivocally that he would always be a stranger to himself. Fact, or wish come true, it becomes the prerequisite for a new identity.

The hero, of course, is a public figure, totally exposed. At the same time, the Resistance was a secret organization and each member received the baptism of a new name.[7] He has his every-

---

7. Camus describes Kierkegaard in the following manner: "Don Juan de la connaissance, il multiplie les pseudonymes" (E, 116). In Algeria, Camus signed

day life but, ideally, it is a perpetual present without the usual hopes for the future or the unexpected intrusions from the past. The future, after all, is death and the past is obscure or troubling. The hero, as a result, does not assume a generational place. His dreams, if he has any, must proclaim his divinity, not his confused humanity, and he must not make any slips of the tongue. At about this time, Camus spelled out the following rule for the artist: "Un écrivain ne doit pas parler de ses doutes en face de sa création. . . . Les doutes, c'est ce que nous avons de plus intime. Ne jamais parler de ses doutes—quels qu'ils soient" (C, 2, 49). The artist, like the hero, cannot share human failings. Committed as he may be, the savior occupies the center of society, all the while remaining alien to it.

The concept of an elitist fraternity which runs through Le Mythe represents Camus' attempt to commit himself to society while surrendering the minimum of the self's domain. Camus is also being quite literal in that fraternity does, in fact, exclude women. When Meursault rejected marriage, he rejected procreation. He wished to remain alien not only to the biological survival of a society but to that sense of continuity wherein we prove to ourselves, through our children, that we are mortal.

A deep sense of mortality sits at the very center of Le Mythe de Sisyphe. Camus condemns Kierkegaard and Jaspers, among many others, who desperately sought an exit from death by believing in immortality. Opposing himself systematically to this doctrine, Camus proposes sterility as an appropriate ideal: "Je ne veux parler . . . que d'un monde où les pensées comme les vies sont privées d'avenir. . . . Dans le monde absurde, la valeur d'une notion ou d'une vie se mesure à son infécondité" (E, 151). He is of course referring to the full incorporation of the fact of death into our physical and mental lives. We also infer from such a statement that fertility as a social and/or religious ideal is futile. Camus' notebooks, particularly between the years of 1942 and 1944, contain numerous derogatory remarks about sexuality and, in their contempt for women, must certainly be labelled misogynist:

---

some of his articles "Mersault," the name of the hero in La Mort heureuse. As a Resistant, Camus also wrote and was known as Bauchard or Mathé.

La vie sexuelle a été donnée à l'homme pour le détourner de sa vraie voie. C'est son opium. En elle tout s'endort. Hors d'elle, les choses reprennent leur vie. En même temps, la chasteté éteint l'espèce, ce qui est peut-être la vérité. (C, 2, 49)[8]

> La sexualité ne mène à rien. Elle n'est pas immorale mais elle est improductive. On peut s'y livrer pour le temps où l'on ne désire pas produire. Mais seule la chasteté est liée à un progrès personnel. (C, 2, 51)

> La femme, hors de l'amour, est ennuyeuse. Elle ne sait pas. Il faut vivre avec l'une et se taire. Ou coucher avec toutes et faire. Le plus important est ailleurs. (C, 2, 58)

Sex and procreativity are linked with dispersion because they constitute an irretrievable loss of independence. Camus devotes an entire chapter of *Le Mythe* to the figure of Don Juan and proposes the amatory hero as another model for the absurd life. His male body, joining with female bodies, produces nothing because nothing of the self will be surrendered. Don Juan only gives enjoyment which has nothing to do with the past or with the future. Among the various versions of Don Juan's death, Camus chooses to see his last days spent in a monastery: "Cela figure . . . le logique aboutissement d'une vie tout entière pénétrée d'absurde, le farouche dénouement d'une existence tournée vers des joies sans lendemain. La jouissance s'achève ici en ascèse" (E, 150). Asceticism is the logical conclusion to promiscuity because, like a kind of metaphysical birth control, it was always there. The onanist cell of Meursault is here replaced by female conquests but sterility remains their common denominator.[9] Had Don Juan produced a child he would have created his own survivor. If one's goal, in Don Juan's words, is "quantity" (E, 154) then a child would be the height of inefficiency. Instead, since Don Juan is both committed to the body and uninvolved,

---

8. When he wrote this, Camus probably had this "pensée" of Pascal in mind: "Mais dira-t-on qui soit bon? La chasteté? Je dis non, car le monde finirait. Le mariage? non: la continence vaut mieux."

9. Raymond Gay-Crosier, in a remarkable study of Camus, offers this insight into Don Juan: "Ainsi commet-il sur le plan de l'amour le même crime que Caligula sur le plan du bonheur." *Les Envers d'un échec; étude sur le théâtre d'Albert Camus* (Paris: Minard, 1967), p. 86.

"le temps," Camus writes, "marche avec lui" (E, 154). The essay has come full circle. Having set out to take his place in time, time now espouses the hero. There is only a present that he alone embodies and everyone else is out of it. At the end of the essay, we are left with the image of Sisyphus, alone, pushing only one rock.

In *Le Mythe de Sisyphe*, Camus stresses the eventual and definitive disappearance of the self. Within this grim context, however, he makes restitution and that restitution in part takes the form of political commitment. Because of that commitment and Camus' renewed emphasis on our place in society, the imperial vision has been literally shot full of holes, allowing for a symbiotic flow of fraternal and even altruistic influences to take place. Yet that same vision, like a flexible organism adopting to foreign circumstances, reemerges with its borders fundamentally intact. The self still remains essentially disengaged because it has become heroic, more than human, able to assume countless identities, as if through sheer excess of energy, and accountable only to itself. History is less a milieu demanding compromise than a decor suitable for intervention. Camus, in this respect, again owes much to the heroic figure Garine who, in Malraux's *Les Conquérants*, does not join the Chinese Revolution to create a more equitable society, but, as he states bluntly to the narrator, to seek and exercise absolute power of life and death over other men. He wants power for the sake of power, the romantic-symbolist aesthetic of "art for art" reincarnated as revolutionary politics. Also paraphrasing Nietzsche, his other master, Camus chooses "l'éternelle vivacité" over "la vie éternelle" (E, 162). Camus' particular accomplishment, therefore, is to turn the doctrine of immortality inside out, to place it in the here and now. The hero, therefore, is more than a superior man; he is a legitimate, that is to say, mortal god. "Secret de mon univers," Camus wrote in his diary, "imaginer Dieu sans l'immortalité humaine" (C, 2, 26). To be a god poses the problem of how to be alone and legion. Referring to Don Juan, Camus states: "Tout être sain tend à se multiplier" (E, 152). In the chapter on conquest we read: "Tout homme s'est senti l'égal d'un dieu à certains moments" (E, 166). Finally, a work of art is described as "la mort d'une expérience et sa multiplication" (E, 174). All three passages describe a resurrection, self-willed and self-induced. Hence they constitute a new synthesis, a fertile sterility. The self, like a work of art, is its own beginning and end. To support this new perspective where immortality is to be achieved in this life, Camus goes so far as to redefine the mission of Christ: "Jésus incarne bien tout le drame humain. Il est l'homme parfait, étant celui qui a réalisé la condition la plus absurde. Il n'est pas le Dieu-homme, mais l'homme-dieu. . . . La divinité dont il s'agit est donc toute terrestre" (E, 184). The following excerpts from Camus' notebooks reinforce his public announcements, offering even more variations on the will to divinity: "L'homme est coupable mais il l'est de n'avoir pas su tout tirer de lui-même" (C, 2, 111); "C'est à nous de créer Dieu. Ce n'est pas lui le créateur. . . . Nous n'avons qu'une façon de créer Dieu, qui est de le devenir" (C, 2, 127). Such affirmations seem to contradict Camus' own numerous references to human limitations such as the inability of reason to formulate absolute truths. The contradiction, however, is only apparent because the emphasis on "frontiers" and "limits" refers to reason specifically and to human mortality in general. Reiterating Ivan Karamazov's "Tout est permis" (E, 149), Camus concludes that life is limitless within the limits of one life. The desire for omnipotence is still present. It sends out its strong charges but this time they spread outward and make up in breadth of experience what they lose in depth and singleness of purpose and even, to some extent, privacy.

Nor does the self that multiplies itself, whether it be through theatrical or political roles, novels, or female conquests, contradict Camus' words, "entrer le plus avant possible dans des vies qui ne sont pas les siennes" (E, 160). Having done so, the result is not cooperation but displacement. Once the self goes elsewhere, once Don Juan has had his satisfaction, that other life ceases to be. The hero-god possesses others the way the young man in *Noces* possessed the sea, without memory. The swimmer, however, trusted the ocean, something outside of himself. Not so, says the author of *Le Mythe*. That ocean was an illusion, a figment of his imagination. His trust was only in himself. But the reader was not offended because the swimmer was young. Henceforth Camus, like Meursault, admits openly that he will not entrust his identity to anything other than himself. Although, unlike Meursault, he renews his vow to society, that vow does not include fidelity, and he multiplies *ad mortem* the heroic personages he will play in order to avoid judgment.

Camus rejected the "grand amour" because it threatened the beloved with annihilation. The interest in Don Juan and his innumerable loves is certainly an attempt to preserve the integrity of the beloved. Since no one woman is singled out, no one is harmed. However, to be sexual but not to be involved also becomes a paradigm of the decision to be political but disengaged. "Faire corps avec" engenders nothing. The goal is to participate but not to experience, not to recognize the full humanity of others who in turn may modify ours. Such recognition would allow individuals not only to make claims on the hero's time but to form moral judgments about his character. Camus claims that if this can be done at all, it can only be done superficially. The more superficial humanity, the more divine Camus' god. The emphasis on relativity enhances the hero's divine status in relationship to the rest of the world because it disposes of formal, objective judgment.

Speaking of the social position of the absurd hero who refuses to accept Christianity, Camus concludes: "On voudrait lui faire connaître sa culpabilité. Lui se sent innocent. A vrai dire, il ne sent que cela, son innocence irréparable. C'est elle qui lui permet tout" (E, 137). The reason Camus contemptuously dismissed both Socrates' "know thyself" and the priest's "be virtuous" is that the former stressed the investigation of personal motives, while the latter made virtue dependent upon human interaction and placed the evaluation of our conduct as much upon others as upon ourselves. In response, Camus exalts will power because its only requirement is that we remain strangers to ourselves. He insists on our innocence because, unlike virtue, it precedes all our acts, and if Camus insists that innocence is inborn and ineradicable, then again, unlike virtue, it need never be demonstrated, much less tested.

The imperial self in *Le Mythe de Sisyphe*, by comparison with that in *L'Etranger*, is participatory, but the terms of its participation are its own. The ideal absurd men are all flamboyant, that is to say public, closer to Caligula in spirit. Meursault himself forsook the dance but Camus is now inviting new audiences to a new performance. The self's dominion, however, has been preserved. What has been modified is the object or particular reality through which the self can exercise and demonstrate its divinity. The ocean in "Noces à Tipasa," Caligula's empire, Meursault's journal have become, in *Le Mythe de Sisyphe*, society. There is in Camus a tremendous sense of his own biography, of his life as a temporal sequence of interrelated and significant events. In these analytical portions of his works, such as the personal essays in *L'Envers et l'endroit* and parts of the *Carnets*, there appear characters such as "la vieille femme" and his own mother who are fleshed out and who capture our attention. Terms like "mauvaise conscience" are also set down and examined. Another impulse in Camus is to be a man without a biography, to be a hero living a succession of present moments without doubt or guilt, in other words without a past. Such contradictions are particularly evident in the *Carnets*. They are rich in information and, at times, extremely revealing about Camus' inner life. They are also contrived. How else could a man write private notebooks and never once refer to his brother, to his membership in the Communist party, or to his marriage and subsequent divorce?

These contradictions are everywhere present but fully realized in *Le Mythe de Sisyphe*. Calling for commitment and confrontation with the world, Camus eventually portrays man confronting himself, not as he is but as he wishes himself to be. He joins us, but as an actor-hero. But where is the human community in all of this? In his own words, Camus chose history over the eternal, action over contemplation, manhood over youth. At the same time, the self, whatever it is, remains more real than any set of political circumstances. The question then arises whether there is really any room for anyone else in such a system because, whether a book, lovers, or political crises, the world becomes a mirror sending images back to Narcissus. Camus does propose commitment and fraternity. There is some cleavage in the monolithic self. It remains for *La Peste* to discover whether a god can live as a hero among men.

3 / *Camus' Discovery of Man*

Comparée à *L'Etranger*, *La Peste* marque, sans discussion possible, le passage d'une attitude de révolte solitaire à la reconnaissance d'une communauté dont il faut partager les luttes. S'il y a évolution de *L'Etranger* à *La Peste*, elle s'est faite dans le sens de la solidarité et de la participation. (TRN, 1973–74)

THESE remarks appear in a letter to Roland Barthes who had suggested that *La Peste* embodied a "morale anti-historique" and a "politique de solitude."[1] Camus wrote his polite but strongly worded letter in 1955. He had already published *L'Homme ré-volté* in which he judged his contemporaries, was preparing *La Chute*, and had traced the direction of his novels, those written and those to come.

The themes of *L'Etranger* and *Le Mythe de Sisyphe* develop outside of time. To quote Camus, both texts stand at "point zéro" (C, 2, 31). Their rejection of the past and future, of memory and hope was in part prompted by a desire to reproduce a tragic vision, the finality of death, in its essential form. It was also willed by an author essaying an image of self, a self that nothing influences and that influences nothing. An awareness of community, however, literary as well as political, while making its presence

1. Camus stresses the theme of community in the letter's conclusion: "J'ai . . . le sentiment de vivre par et pour une communauté" (TRN, 1975).

felt in some of the statements and preoccupations of *Le Mythe*, emerges fully and most forcefully in *La Peste*.

From 1941 to 1947, the composition of *La Peste* spanned six crucial years in Camus' life. He joined the Resistance; saw the publication of *L'Etranger* (1942) and *Le Mythe de Sisyphe* (1943) which conferred upon him immediate, international fame; took over the direction of the left-wing newspaper *Combat* in 1944, making it the finest and most responsible newspaper of the post-war period; commenced work on *L'Homme révolté*; and, in 1947, left *Combat* because of internal dissension among the editors and because financial difficulties would have made it necessary to sacrifice quality and independence for a larger circulation.[2]

In his editorials Camus stresses his conviction that the fraternity he had discovered in the Resistance could be extended into peacetime and become the vehicle for social revolution. Camus' well-known interest in sports is given wider and more ambitious scope when he looks first to his companions in the Resistance and then to his colleagues in *Combat* to mold a new society. The fraternity he described in *Le Mythe de Sisyphe* looks ahead to the Resistance, but it also reincarnates his teammates and the group of authors, himself included, who had collaborated on *Révolte dans les Asturies*. After the publication of *La Peste*, Camus worked closely with Jean-Louis Barrault on *L'Etat de siège*, an allegorical dramatization of a plague in Cadiz, Spain and his second attempt at communal theatre.

Part of the power that we find in Camus' editorials during this particular period stems from his belief that the world had been destroyed and that it was necessary to start again, to be a creator in the political sphere. The world no longer had a past. It was a propitious time to create a future. Whereas in *Le Mythe* he had condemned contemplation and the future as evasions from an urgent present, he now states in 1946: "Ce qui frappe le plus . . . dans le monde où nous vivons, c'est . . . que la plupart des hommes . . . sont privés d'avenir. Il n'y a pas de vie valable sans projection sur l'avenir, sans promesse de mûrissement et de progrès" (E, 331). The Nazis were defeated and Europe, Phoenix-like, had to be reborn. A word like "progress" that would have

2. E, 1503–5.

been anathema to the author of *Le Mythe de Sisyphe* finds favor with the editor of *Combat*. A world that does not end obviously requires a new ethic. The essay on Sisyphus banished God and replaced him with an exalted self espousing an apocalypse. Now in peacetime the self by itself is found wanting. As early as 1944 Camus had written to the literary critic Guy Dumur:

> Une des rares choses que je sache aujourd'hui c'est que nous ne sommes pas seuls. Il y a la parole et l'écriture, l'amour, la haine ou la violence, aucun de nous n'est désert ni silence absolu. . . . Quant à ce sentiment de solitude qu'on éprouve authentiquement, il vient peut-être de ce qu'on délaisse les hommes et qu'on s'adresse à ce qui ne peut pas répondre, c'est-à-dire à soi-même ou à quelque puissance inconnue. . . . Je suppose qu'il faut choisir: la solitude avec Dieu ou l'histoire avec les hommes. . . . Il me semble que j'ai choisi. Aucune vérité ne me paraît valable si elle n'est pas atteinte à travers les êtres, je ne crois pas à la solitude. (E, 1670–71)

Camus had said as much in *Le Mythe* but the emphases were different, more on the inevitability of solitude, less on the freedom of choice. There too Camus had rejected God but not the solitude with himself. The hero's commitment went so far as an artist or actor facing his public, a populated solitude. "History with men" means much more during and after the Resistance than before. It now has the weight of experience and of compromise. The imperial self is an unauthored self, but now a fraternity exists where, through dialogue, the self draws sustenance, in turn sustaining.

A year earlier, writing to the poet Francis Ponge to praise his book, *Le Parti pris des choses*, Camus had remarked: "Prendre conscience—nous avons pour cela besoin les uns des autres" (E, 1667). In order to preserve his indifference Meursault systematically avoided, not the physical presence of other people, but their mental or emotional intrusions, whether they took the form of marriage, that is to say, of something more than sex, or the inevitable probes of a sustained dialogue. Others could be present provided they were absent. He kills the Arab but the shots awaken him only to his own death wish. In contrast, *La Peste* is rich in dialogue, confrontations, and confessions. Camus also reaffirms in the *Carnets* the connection between dialogue and social consciousness: "Ce qui équilibre l'absurde c'est la communauté des hommes en lutte contre lui. Et si nous choisissons de servir cette communauté nous choisissons de servir le dialogue jusqu'à l'absurde contre toute politique du mensonge ou du silence" (C, 2, 162). These remarks support what soon becomes evident in *La Peste*, that the community is no longer the middleman between the hero and the absurd waiting, like an audience, to applaud or perhaps disapprove, that the community has absorbed the hero and now requires his services on an equal basis in the creation of a new and more just society. In an editorial of 1944 Camus formulates the fundamental axiom of his postwar politics: "La justice pour tous, c'est la soumission de la personnalité au bien collectif" (E, 271).

Camus tells us that life in occupied France was, at worst, a succession of "monologues stériles," at best a "dialogue d'ombres" (E, 299). The secret, often silent fraternity of resistants, however, was transformed after the Liberation into a union of visible and committed men, into debate and open dialogue. Camus' decision immediately after the war to collect and preface the poems of René Leynaud,[3] a devout Catholic, resistant and very close friend killed by the Gestapo in 1943 was, among other things, an attempt to make an unknown person known. The transformation of *Combat* from underground weapon to public newspaper, of Camus himself from obscure combatant to celebrated writer encouraged this sense of ties openly avowed and of mutual cooperation. The pseudonyms Camus had used in Algeria and during the Occupation could now be erased. Henceforth, Camus would use his own name or, more significant, none at all when, as it often happened, the editorial staff shared the same view. Such a practice did not result in anonymity. It demonstrated instead a vital team spirit.

As editor Camus will never cease to propose dialogue as the stylistic basis for moral and political reform. What he now dreads is the indifference Meursault practiced and which threatens even Sisyphus, the apparently logical reaction to the insignificance of life. In the same letter to Ponge:

3. E, 1471–79.

L'homme, chez vous, cherche . . . sa parenté avec le monde. Et en réalité, quoique vous vous dirigiez vers le relativisme humain . . . il y a dans vos textes poétiques un message plus catégorique et moins conciliant. J'y découvre les signes de ce qui, aujourd'hui, me préoccupe et me presse: qu'une des fins de la réflexion absurde est l'indifférence et le renoncement total—celui de la pierre. . . . Sisyphe devient alors rocher lui-même. . . . En fait, il y a dans votre pensée, comme dans toute pensée absurde, la nostalgie de l'immobilité. (E, 1664–65)

By writing this letter Camus is able to reread his own book and, by forming certain critical judgments, measure his own evolution. What he considered, however, a latent possibility of the absurdist premises in *Le Mythe*, namely indifference, was in fact already manifest. Its heroes move and appear vital, but because time stands still for them that movement becomes an artist's illusion, a metaphysical *trompe-l'oeil*. In his letter Camus describes the absurd self as a stone idol, a deity immobilized in silence, a male version of Baudelaire's "rêve de pierre" and perhaps of his own mother. Camus comments many times that his mother was mute, partially deaf, and apparently indifferent. It would not be too hazardous to speculate that her child would wonder if either of them was truly alive. His monologues to her would not be sterile if they were attempts to awaken feelings and to be nourished by them in turn. Under different circumstances they would indeed be sterile were the mother to become, as Camus himself suspected, a model for his conduct in society. Meursault's own first person narration, for example, does not prompt responses or provide cues for dialogue. His monologue, which is written, is suicidal because it creates its own desert, his personal solution to the aesthetic problem of how to talk and remain silent, to be and not to be like his mother.

La Peste reveals more positive ambitions. Going one step further than *L'Étranger*, Camus now finds the self unwilling or unable to engage only in soliloquy. Camus told Guy Dumur that we are not alone and that history and commitment were the opposites of solitude and silence. If the self cannot or should not talk to itself, then its friends will and by their verbal cues prompt it to action. Silence is still important but there are two kinds: the silence of a passive spirit which must be broken; the partial silence that must be imposed on a self prone to monologue, to acting alone. Dialogue satisfies both exigencies. As Camus points out: "Nous avons à retrouver notre banalité" (E, 1682). Banality, our commonness, has to be found again because either it was lost or else never existed. In 1944, analyzing Brice Parain's study of language entitled "Sur une philosophie de l'expression,"[4] Camus quotes with complete approval this description of the function of language: "'Sa destination est de formuler ce que l'homme a de plus strictement impersonnel, de plus intimement pareil aux autres.' C'est à cette banalité supérieure que peut-être il faut se tenir, là où se rejoignent l'artiste et l'homme des champs, le penseur et l'ouvrier" (E, 1679). Impersonality is the antithesis of monologue but it is not the same thing as dialogue where strongly identifiable individuals interact and modify each other's views. Dialogue, however, can effect a transition from the conflict of opposing views to agreement, concord, and a common ground for action.

Consequently, impersonality is the antithesis of both monologue and anonymity. It would embody a political order, if not of equality, perhaps of fraternity. To Parain's general description Camus adds a cast of characters, the artist and thinker working hand in hand with the worker and farmer. He has radically modified the privileged status of the conquerors in *Le Mythe de Sisyphe*. After urging that we rediscover our banality, he added: "La question est seulement de savoir si nous aurons à la fois le génie et le coeur simple qu'il y faut" (E, 1682). Much depends on how Camus will answer that question.

Impersonality is viable because the Resistance had demonstrated to Camus that there were truths for which men were willing to sacrifice their lives, that something transcended the individual. The fissures in the monolithic self we observed in *Le Mythe* are opening further to reveal a community. From the point of view of successfully delineated characters who possess truly human dimensions, *La Peste* is Camus' most populated novel. It satisfies us differently from *L'Etranger* and *La Chute* because it possesses a dense, social space. One year after praising

4. TRN, 1936.

Parain's theory of the communal basis of language, Camus published "Remarque sur la révolte" in which he turns his attention from the individual to the group:

C'est dans la révolte que l'homme se dépasse dans autrui. . . . Dans l'expérience absurde, la tragédie est individuelle. A partir du mouvement de révolte, elle a conscience d'être collective. Elle est l'aventure de tous. Le premier progrès d'un esprit saisi d'étrangeté est de reconnaître qu'il partage cette étrangeté avec tous les hommes et que la réalité humaine dans sa totalité souffre de cette distance par rapport à soi et au monde. Le mal qu'éprouvait jusque-là un seul homme devient peste collective. (E, 1685)

At most, *Le Mythe de Sisyphe*, which had been on Camus' mind as early as 1938, exalted an heroic elite that consented to serve the masses. In his letters and study of Parain, in his editorials and essays during the period just prior to and immediately after the Liberation, Camus' thinking becomes increasingly collectivistic. Meursault and Sisyphus are no longer alone. Camus was even considering entitling his second novel *Les Prisonniers*. Whereas Meursault considered "others" to be an obstacle to his own self-possession, whereas the absurd hero granted others the status of victim or audience, mere mirrors of his purpose, now, through the experience of war, Camus, separated from his second wife during most of the Occupation, in revolt against Nazism and working in the Resistance network, has discovered other strangers. Self-absorption gradually gives way to multiple loyalties. Because of Nazism the division of one against many in *L'Etranger*, the contract of one with many in *Le Mythe de Sisyphe*, becomes, in the war and later in *La Peste*, the opposition of Europe against a massive totalitarian machine. The four *Lettres à un ami allemand* Camus wrote between 1943 and 1944 are extremely significant in this respect because he attributes to his Nazi "friend" ideas he had himself expressed in *Le Mythe de Sisyphe*:

Vous n'avez jamais cru au sens de ce monde et vous en avez tiré l'idée que tout était équivalent et que le bien et le mal se définissait selon qu'on le voulait. Vous avez supposé qu'en l'absence de toute morale humaine ou divine les seules valeurs étaient celles qui régissaient le monde animal, c'est-à-dire la violence et la ruse . . . que dans la plus insensée des histoires la tâche d'un individu ne pouvait être que l'aventure de la puissance, et sa morale, le réalisme des conquêtes. Et à la vérité, moi qui croyais penser comme vous, je ne voyais guère d'argument à vous opposer, sinon un goût violent de la justice qui, pour finir, me paraissait aussi peu raisonné que la plus soudaine des passions. (E, 240)

Camus is saying what Caligula said to himself before his death, that the premise of life's total insignificance, particularly the devaluation of human life and of ethics, leads toward two contradictory decisions: either to incarnate that insignificance or to create significant values. The latter is preferable because it assumes that the discovery of insignificance demonstrates significance, the ability to articulate rationally what is irrational in the world. The absurd hero reconciled this contradiction insofar as he thought he could enjoy the divine status he willed for himself in the absence of all moral limits without inflicting harm. On the contrary, he would liberate the oppressed. The war itself made that precarious balance untenable. Crises simplify. Camus now thrusts man and himself midway between tyrants and gods and confers both roles upon the Nazis. "Qu'est-ce que l'homme," he asks in his second letter and he responds: "Il est cette force qui finit toujours par balancer les tyrans et les dieux" (E, 228). Camus now wants to be a man among men and *La Peste* will examine that ambition.

Until now Camus' fiction spoke essentially to the dilemma of man's solitude, a solitude conferred by certain death and by personal choice, as well as the emotional solitude into which Camus seems to have been born. It may be idealized in *L'Etranger* or else in "Noces à Tipasa" where it swells into a diapason of an expanding self; or it is modified to include other gods as in *Le Mythe de Sisyphe*. Encoded in Camus' fiction, however, is not only the theme of solitude but the problem of its literary expression. One solution in *L'Etranger* (and later in *La Chute*) is first person narration. When, on the contrary, Camus examines human solidarity, the monologue as a stylistic and moral option is abandoned in favor of a more traditional third person narrative structure employing dialogue.

Meursault seems to be sincere, to be objective, when he reproduces speeches of other characters as well as those verbal exchanges in which he himself participates. The reader soon realizes, however, that such objectivity, while appearing to enrich the text with multiple points of view, is less an active and positive choice of the hero and more a manifestation of his indifference to human life. The following exchanges with the priest are not untypical:

"Pourquoi . . . refusez-vous mes visites?" J'ai répondu que je ne croyais pas en Dieu. (TRN, 1207)

"Comment aborderez-vous cette terrible épreuve?" J'ai répondu que je l'aborderais exactement comme je l'abordais en ce moment. (TRN, 1208)

The following exchange is between Meursault and Marie:

"Pourquoi m'épouser alors?" a-t-elle dit. Je lui ai expliqué que cela n'avait aucune importance. (TRN, 1156)

This alternation between direct quotes and indirect statements, given the context of Meursault's avowed indifference, emphasizes the gap between the characters. Since it is Meursault who is writing in the first person, he has effectively neutralized those other points of view. Hence his status as solitary stranger. Camus tells us that Meursault only answers questions.[5] I would add that, because of his frequent use of indirect statement, Meursault answers the question only, never the person who asks and whose question falls into an emotional vacuum. The questions jut into but do not impede the flow of his narrative. In contrast, the objectivity of Bernard Rieux, doctor and principal character of *La Peste*, dramatizes his commitment to protect human life, particularly in the form of free expression. To guarantee that freedom, the narration is in the third person with the emphasis on dialogue. As the character Joseph Grand admits: "J'ai confiance en vous. Avec vous, je peux parler" (TRN, 1286).[6]

5. C, 2, 19.
6. Similarly, Rambert:

The narrative structure of *La Peste* corresponds to the political concerns of Camus' editorials. Those concerns were not static and Roger Quilliot observes two stages: from 1944 to 1945; 1945 to 1948.[7] The first stage would represent Camus' attempts to extend the clandestine activities of the Resistance into political revolution; the second would see efforts to modify the term "revolution" and to set limits to political action specifically and to the dominion of history in general. Quilliot's dates are, I think, debatable but the development he observes in Camus' thinking is undeniably there.

Those limits are closely related to Camus' interest in impersonality and dialogue and to the narrative form he adopts for *La Peste*. The conflicts in Camus between solitude and commitment, monologue and dialogue, self and others are always present. In 1944, for example, we heard him praise Parain's statement that the highest form of language is "strictement impersonnel." What happens, however, when impersonality becomes systematic, when it ceases to describe the final outcome of debate and begins to prescribe initial attitudes? In 1943, in the article "L'Intelligence et l'échafaud," Camus himself was already on his guard: "Il faut s'oublier à moitié au profit d'une expression communicable" (TRN, 1897). Camus was trying in this meditation on Madame de Lafayette to formulate a contemporary classicism and the results of his efforts are visible in the style he eventually adopted for *La Peste*. That classicism, based on a sound balance between the self's private, often obscure, constellation of linguistic signs and symbols and the public domain of conventional intelligibility, has its political variant when Camus confronts the individual with his historical circumstances and political responsibilities. The following comment on French art from the same article might come under the general heading of aesthetics but only in part: "Nous sommes très fiers de l'universalité de notre goût. Mais elle détend peut-être notre force intérieure" (TRN, 1901). Interpreted politically, this statement illuminates Camus' dilemma, particularly intense between 1943

—Tarrou, dit le journaliste, je voudrais voir le docteur. Excusez-moi.
—Je sais. Il est plus humain qui moi (TRN, 1387).
7. E, 1571.

and 1947, whether politics is omnipresent, if not totalitarian in its demands, and whether the artist, in offering his entire allegiance to the historical enterprise of revolution and the community that embodies it, going so far as to praise Parain's quasi-monastic impersonality, is not in fact diluting his creative powers, his language, and his self. Would not the monolithic, political "group" merely represent a more socially acceptable version of the monolithic "ego?" Camus summarized this conflict in 1945:

> Si le classicisme se définit par la domination des passions, une époque classique est celle dont l'art met en formes et en formules les passions des contemporains. Aujourd'hui où les passions collectives ont pris le pas sur les passions individuelles, ce n'est plus l'amour qu'il s'agit de dominer par l'art, mais la politique. . . .
>
> Mais combien la tâche est plus difficile—(1) parce que, s'il faut vivre les passions avant de les formuler, la passion collective dévore tout le temps de l'artiste; (2) parce que les chances de mort y sont plus grandes—et que même, c'est la seule manière de vivre authentiquement la passion collective, que d'accepter de mourir pour elle. Ici donc, la plus grande chance d'authenticité est également la plus grande chance d'échec pour l'art. (C, 2, 144)

Camus wishes to examine carefully what happens when the writer discovers that politics are as soul-consuming as the woman's love he described in *Le Mythe*. Whereas grammar can become a *modus vivendi* between writer and reader in the realm of intelligibility, can politics, the collective passion of the twentieth century, offer similar guarantees as the writer seeks to reconcile his public and private lives?

The narrative structure of *La Peste* went through two distinct stages which correspond to the adjustments Camus brought to the doctrine of collectivist politics. In its first version of 1943 the novel consisted of the journals of Doctor Rieux, Stephan, a teacher abandoned by his wife and who eventually commits suicide, and of Jean Tarrou. Interspersed among these three entries were newspaper reports, statistics, and other relevant documents. Such an outline demonstrates Camus' concern with impersonality to the extent that an aesthetic equality reigns in these separate journals with no one voice allowed to dominate, an aesthetic equivalent of a Resistance network. This structure is designed to encourage a fraternity of writers, and Camus must also have recalled his collaborative efforts with three other companions to write *Révolte dans les Asturies* for the "Théâtre du Travail," a theater group sponsored by the Communist party. In the second version Camus gradually abandons Stephan altogether, putting in his place the secondary character of Joseph Grand, and he transfers many of Stephan's preoccupations with the theme of love to a new character, the journalist Raymond Rambert. Rieux's journals are no longer identified as such. It is now Rieux, adopting a posture of strict objectivity, who narrates all the events that take place in the novel, including at regular intervals the testimony of Tarrou's journal, relevant portions of which he alone selects and incorporates into his book. The narrator, however, is not anonymous since he informs the reader of his intentions to identify himself at the end. As a result, he may temporarily not have a name but he most assuredly has a presence. The unidentified narrator, therefore, speaks directly to the reader in the form of "je" and refers to Rieux, to himself, as "il." By this means, Camus has demonstrated his belief in impersonality and classical objectivity out of which arise several distinct voices and a principal character. He has also created a hierarchy and through that hierarchy the unity one narrator alone can provide, the unity of a single point of view, objective in its fidelity to facts, subjective in its exercise of choice. That subjectivity represents what Camus owes to his art and to his personal freedom. This second and definitive version represents the stylistic equivalent of a moral option, a compromise between self-interest and the domination of politics that Camus called "s'oublier à moitié." Impersonality alone could go too far in the direction of self-denial.

Rieux's book, moreover, unlike Meursault's, was undertaken for the avowed purpose of publication, for the creation of human ties. He would reject the status of hero but not the status of a man who was a participant, a doctor, and who is now an artist enriching a collective effort with his own biography. Camus has therefore reconciled two antithetical but, in his view, equally valid exigencies which he summarized succinctly in the article

"Révolte et servitude": "Sous la forme d'une chronique objective écrite à la troisième personne, *La Peste* est une confession" (E, 758).

Given the importance of the related themes of fraternity, dialogue, and political revolution, the shift from a book organized around separate journals to one organized around a single narrator was audacious, so much so that it prompted Camus to justify his decision. Firstly, and by way of compensation, the narrator refuses to identify himself. Only at the end does he divulge his identity. Secondly, Rieux's willingness to narrate is based on a viewpoint that reaffirms certain psychological and aesthetic assumptions:

> Pour être un témoin fidèle, il [le narrateur] devait rapporter surtout les actes, les documents, et les rumeurs. Mais ce que, personnellement, il avait à dire, son attente, ses épreuves, il devait les taire. . . . Quand il se trouvait tenté de mêler directement sa confidence aux mille voix des pestiférés, il était arrêté par la pensée qu'il n'y avait pas une de ses souffrances qui ne fût en même temps celle des autres et que dans un monde où la douleur est si souvent solitaire, cela était un avantage. Décidément, il devait parler pour tous. (TRN, 1468–69)

Camus seems to take for granted one of the fundamental axioms of fiction from the Renaissance to romanticism, that the writer and his public share a common fund of experience justifying the use of "je." The Occupation was just such an experience. The fact that Camus refers systematically to "les autres" instead of "je" in no way invalidates this profound sense of community. If anything, it reinforces it. "Je" is not denied. It associates itself completely with a collectivity and at the same time makes itself heard. Camus gradually realized, however, how precarious and optimistic such an assumption became in postwar France. It would be instructive to read an excerpt from Victor Hugo's preface to *Les Contemplations* because, even in 1857, all the while reaffirming the coidentity of the poet and public, Hugo is acutely aware of a bond rapidly dissolving:

> Est-ce donc la vie d'un homme? Oui, et la vie des autres hommes aussi. Nul de nous n'a l'honneur d'avoir une vie qui soit à lui. Ma vie est

la vôtre, votre vie est la mienne, vous vivez ce que je vis; la destinée est une. Prenez donc ce miroir, et regardez-vous-y. On se plaint quelquefois des écrivains qui disent "moi." Parlez-nous de nous, leur crie-t-on. Hélas! quand je vous parle de moi, je vous parle de vous. Comment ne le sentez-vous pas? Ah! insensé qui crois que je ne suis pas toi.[8]

Camus has reversed Hugo's terms. Since he says "vous" in *La Peste*, there is no need to say "je." It goes without saying. An objective chronicle equals a confession; a confession an objective chronicle. For all that, are we in fact dealing with an equation? If "vous" is the same as "je," then why feel uncomfortable, if not guilty, according to the communist press of the time, when saying "je"? While writing *La Peste*, Camus made the following notes: "La renaissance est dans le désintéressement" (C, 2, 92); "Il faut supprimer le miroir" (C, 2, 94). Years later he reviewed his creative output in the following terms: "Depuis mes premiers livres jusqu'à . . . *L'Homme révolté*, tout mon effort a été de me dépersonnaliser . . . je me suis efforcé à l'objectivité, contraire à ma nature" (C, 2, 267). His efforts at total commitment, as he himself recognized, are impeded by the mirror, his Narcissism, and by his fundamental distrust and fear, amounting almost to paranoia, of psychic dispersion through sex, of any form whatsoever of human contact, misanthropy compounded by misogyny. It is not a question of an equation, therefore, but of an equilibrium, that is to say, of perpetual tension. The co-identity between "I" and "you" has long since ceased to be an assumption. It is something that has to be won and sustained. Whenever Camus feels intense disgust with himself and his vices, political commitment promises salvation. When he judges that Narcissism is not necessarily synonymous with privacy, individualism, and creativity, he sets limits to the "revolution" and collective passions. *La Peste* started out by tipping the balance in favor of politics and selflessness only, at midpoint, to be suddenly redressed.

Many chapters of *La Peste* analyze the effects of the plague upon the citizens of Oran. It is described as an unexpected in-

8. "Préface," *Les Contemplations* (Bourges: Garnier, 1957), p. 4.

vasion and the book owes part of its power to the then recent experience of Nazism. The descriptions of a terrified city at night, the blackmarket, the forced separations, the burial of victims, all these translate historical events. *La Peste*, as a result, has acquired the severe status of a social document.

The shift of Camus' attention away from the self to the group causes him to abandon the heroic mold in which he had cast *Le Mythe de Sisyphe*. He had already concluded in the fourth and last of the *Lettres à un ami allemand*, written in 1944, that "l'héroïsme est peu de chose" (E, 242). Both *Le Mythe* and *La Peste* share the same tragic vision. Heroism, however, as a mode of self-validation is now unacceptable to Camus for the same reason that gave rise to his heroic views in the first place, the spectacle of mass suffering. The concretion of human energies in one man alone, at a time when solidarity is essential to survival, would leave the community too dependent in peacetime as well as in war.

Camus goes so far as to parody the traditional hero, the "stranger in town" who conquers evil and then leaves. Raymond Rambert is trapped by the quarantine and he makes every imaginable effort to leave the plague-ridden city in order to rejoin the woman he loves. That fidelity to one woman is already a correction to the chapter on Don Juan in *Le Mythe de Sisyphe*. When Rambert does decide to remain he becomes part of a sanitation team. He states categorically: "Je ne crois pas à l'héroïsme" (TRN, 1351). His reason is significant. Heroism, he asserts, is "meurtrier" (TRN, 1351). Rieux echoes this same sentiment and his ultimate justification for giving heroism, at best, "la place secondaire" (TRN, 1331) lies in the murderous equation that obtains between "belles actions" and "un hommage indirect et puissant au mal" (TRN, 1326). Heroism exists to fight evil and evil in turn furnishes the hero with his sole reason for being. A war, by this declension, becomes an unholy alliance. Rambert argues for the private life, for the pursuit of happiness and, since he is in love, for a kind of dual egotism. It is his sexual élan that is thwarted and ultimately redirected by the plague. Although Rambert finds an escape route from the city, he decides to stay precisely because Rieux has become, meanwhile, a model of self-sacrifice, the antithesis to heroic self-aggrandizement.

Rieux proposes instead that we accept as the book's "hero" Joseph Grand, an insignificant clerk long since abandoned by his wife, who works for Rieux, and whose personal goal is to write a great novel:

S'il est vrai que les hommes tiennent à se proposer des exemples et des modèles qu'ils appellent héros, et s'il faut absolument qu'il y en ait un dans cette histoire, le narrateur propose justement ce héros insignifiant et effacé qui n'avait pour lui qu'un peu de bonté au coeur et un idéal apparemment ridicule. (TRN, 1331)

Because he is insignificant Grand's heroism will disappear with the plague. His virtue will not conjure up another vice. He does not proclaim his heroism because he is unaware of it, unaware too that he has been proposed for our admiration. To the extent, therefore, that the characters in *La Peste* such as Rieux, Rambert, and Grand are unheroic, Camus has abandoned a distinguishing feature of his imperial vision.

Jean Tarrou is also a stranger in Oran but his presence disturbs the premises of solidarity developed in the novel. Through this particular personage the clear opposition of the group against the plague becomes blurred. Since he is both an attractive as well as menacing figure, the reader acquires a more relativistic view of the plague and its identity. Rieux, and Camus through Rieux, give him much attention.

No one in the novel can say where he comes from or why he lives in Oran. He has no visible means of support and he is always found "dans tous les endroits publics" (TRN, 1235). For most of the duration of the plague Tarrou has no biography. His presence, consequently, is that much more miraculous, free as it is from any definable past and those inevitable limitations that attend all *curricula vitae*. We are told that Tarrou is omnipresent,[9] and he himself tells us he is omniscient.[10] It is logical, therefore, that Rieux calls him "l'historien de ce qui n'a pas d'histoire" (TRN, 1236). Omniscience does not necessarily exclude

---

9. Camus, opposing the body to the soul's eternal life, had written in *Le Mythe de Sisyphe*: "Entre 'partout' et 'toujours,' il n'y a pas de compromis" (E, 162).

10. "Oui, Rieux, je sais tout de la vie, vous le voyez bien" (TRN, 1425). In *Ré-*

history or politics. Rather, it turns its attention by preference to the universal because whatever has no history either never existed or does not change. When Tarrou studies whatever has no history, he is studying whatever resembles his own nature, either as it is or as he wishes it to be.

Tarrou does eventually divulge his past to Rieux. It is not the plague alone that prompts Tarrou to this act. By his own admission he has, for the first time, formed ties with someone other than his mother. His revelations seal his friendship with Rieux. Tarrou's biography is organized around two profound shocks: the realization that his loving father had condemned many men to death in his capacity as prosecuting attorney; and the discovery that he himself, after identifying with the victims and joining radical groups, has also ended up, like his father, condemning men to death. These two revelations explain Tarrou's assertion: "Je souffrais déjà de la peste bien avant de connaître cette ville et cette épidémie" (TRN, 1420). Tarrou, therefore, will henceforth live his life at attention, that is to say, according to the precepts that Camus himself set down in *Le Mythe de Sisyphe*. His view is that the plague is not only an historical circumstance or sickness of the body, but an inner, permanent disposition to kill. The reasons for killing are secondary, as if human consciousness, bordered by other existences, cannot tolerate proximity. Tarrou's solution to that disposition which, as the son of his father, he has discovered in himself, is to exercise absolute self-control:

Chacun la porte en soi, la peste, parce que personne, non, personne au monde n'en est indemne. Il faut se surveiller sans arrêt pour ne pas être amené, dans une minute de distraction, à respirer dans la figure d'un autre et à lui coller l'infection. Ce qui est naturel, c'est le microbe. Le reste, la santé, l'intégrité, la pureté, si vous voulez, c'est un effet de la volonté et d'une volonté qui ne doit jamais s'arrêter. . . . A partir du moment où j'ai renoncé à tuer, je me suis condamné à un exil définitif. Ce sont les autres qui feront l'histoire. (TRN, 1425–26)

---

flexions sur la guillotine, Camus wrote: "Qui croit tout savior imagine tout pouvoir" (E, 1060).

This revelation appears in a novel whose characters are engaged in saving lives. There is optimism as well as agony in Tarrou's enterprise of total lucidity because Tarrou firmly believes, as Camus once believed, that the will can exercise such control and that the will remains the only innocence a man can achieve after his fall.

Tarrou's self-control coexists with his extreme gregariousness, the latter a necessary condition if control is at all times to be demonstrated. Consequently, as a hero of will power who is himself his own conquest, he finds in the plague his greatest enemy and surest ally. His ambition is to be a "meurtrier innocent" (TRN, 1426), that is to say, guilty by nature but innocent in deed. Resembling Meursault at the moment he killed the Arab, it would never occur to Tarrou to blame the sun. By comparison, Meursault seems pre-moral, a child, since he considers himself guilty in fact but innocent by nature. Tarrou relates that, before he knew his father, he lived his life believing in his innate innocence. Camus has here transposed, almost word for word, a personal confession from the *Carnets*: "J'ai vécu toute ma jeunesse avec l'idée de mon innocence, c'est-à-dire avec pas d'idée du tout. Aujourd'hui . . ." (C, 2, 154).[11] That abrupt halt is eloquent. Camus is also comparing Tarrou's description of acquired or reacquired innocence with his other claim to innate innocence in *Le Mythe de Sisyphe*. That claim coincided with a call to heroism under the banner of "Tout est permis." Lucidity and will are also extolled in *Le Mythe* but as guarantors of sexual and political adventures. The heroes of *Le Mythe* overwhelm everything and everyone. In Tarrou's case lucidity and will are inducted for the purpose of self-control, the fear of infecting. They prevent human contact. Paradoxically, the result is almost the same in both cases. Active or passive, the imperial self remains fundamentally intact. Tarrou, at least, has a friend in Rieux. He also knows he has a higher ambition, to be, as he puts it, a saint without God. Such sanctity seems a contradiction in terms until we realize that Tarrou wants to contrive his life more than live it, that his desire to be a saint without God translates his decision to

---

11. Tarrou says: "Quand j'étais jeune, je vivais avec l'idée de mon innocence, c'est-à-dire avec pas d'idée du tout" (TRN, 1420).

have, like the heroes of *Le Mythe*, neither a past nor a future, and never to entrust his identity to anyone. Tarrou is attractive because he in part fails. Deceived by his father he no longer trusts preexistent models, not even God. Deceived by himself he can still pay attention to himself, if not recreate himself *ex nihilo*. He offers his biography but only to demolish it. Rieux also hears Tarrou admit his limitations bluntly:

"Je me sens plus de solidarité avec les vaincus qu'avec les saints. Je n'ai pas de goût, je crois, pour l'héroïsme et la sainteté. Ce qui m'intéresse, c'est d'être un homme.
    Oui, nous cherchons la même chose, mais je suis moins ambitieux." (TRN, 1427)

That admission, perhaps more than anything else, calls attention to Camus' efforts to shift the center of gravity from the imperial to the human dimensions that Rieux is meant to incarnate. He becomes the normal man by which we judge the other characters. He also represents a remarkable admission on the part of Camus, given his many references to innocence and to the simple heart, that one can do good and be evil, that politics, no matter how noble, does not automatically grant diplomas of virtue, and, conversely, that a predisposition to kill does not rule out commitment and responsibility. What counts is the pragmatic *hic et nunc*.

The question then arises whether Tarrou's desire for sanctity is as "murderous" as heroism. If not murderous, does his sanctity at least profit from the plague? One answer is possible if we look at Tarrou's other companion, Cottard.

If Joseph Grand is proposed to us as a hero, then the closest equivalent to a villain would be Cottard. A criminal, he welcomes the plague as a means of escaping the police whose efforts are now entirely directed towards the preservation of order. He becomes a black marketeer. At the same time, he tries to acquire through his conduct with neighbors and acquaintances, conduct as meticulously planned as a script, a reputation for virtue in the event of future prosecution. More precisely, he seeks to maintain a reputation already conferred upon him by the plague.

Though a minor character in the book, Cottard is a major

character in the journal of Tarrou. Rieux carefully notes this fact:

> Les notes de Tarrou . . . convergent peu à peu sur le personnage de Cottard. Tarrou a essayé de donner un tableau des réactions et des réflexions de Cottard. . . . Sous la rubrique "Rapports de Cottard et de la peste," ce tableau occupe quelques pages du carnet. . . . L'opinion générale de Tarrou . . . se résumait dans ce jugement: "C'est un personnage qui grandit." (TRN, 1377)

By a kind of moral symbiosis, Cottard thrives on the plague whose devastation grants him the liberty to be a criminal with impunity. On the subject of the plague Cottard customarily replies: "Parlez toujours, je l'ai eue avant vous" (TRN, 1378). Tarrou himself says: "Je souffrais déjà de la peste bien avant de connaître cette ville." The tone is certainly not the same and Tarrou does fight the plague. He is setting up, however, through parallelism, a moral hyphen linking him to this criminal.[12] Without ceasing to be guilty both men are able to contrive their innocence within the context of evil. Tarrou's anguish and sense of guilt leave Cottard's petty plots far behind, but both men, each in his own way, find in this all-enfolding and democratic plague the means to devise and demonstrate an identity of their choice. Tarrou and Cottard, like the actors in Le Mythe, are personages rather than persons, absurdist characters in a post-absurdist novel.

The dependency of each individual upon the plague is underlined as the intensity of the plague begins to subside. Cottard becomes panic-stricken and ends up shooting into a crowd of people from an upper story window. The journal of Tarrou, like the plague, becomes increasingly disorganized:

> A vrai dire, ces carnets deviennent assez bizarres à partir du moment où les statistiques commencent à baisser. Est-ce la fatigue, mais l'écriture en devient difficilement lisible et l'on passe trop souvent d'un sujet à l'autre. De plus, et pour la première fois, ces carnets manquent à

---

12. Just as Rambert and Grand feel comfortable speaking to Rieux, Cottard prefers to speak to Tarrou: "Avec celui-là, avait dit Cottard à Rambert, on peut causer, parce que c'est un homme. On est toujours compris" (TRN, 1377).

l'objectivité et font place à des considérations personnelles. (TRN, 1445)

In his heroic dedication to absolute self-awareness, Tarrou does not, could not take into consideration mere fatigue, the limits of a human nature. The plague charged him with the supplementary energy to maintain himself at the highest point of tension. That current gone, Tarrou loses the inspiration that only his enemy could give him. When the plague withdraws Cottard and Tarrou disintegrate, the former into his status as criminal, the other into subjectivity, into a state of confused humanity. They become persons again. Cottard is apprehended by the police and the omniscient Tarrou dies.

Through Tarrou the plague is internalized. More than a physical disease, it is a disposition to kill, to be a murderous god. The structure of *L'Etranger* was organized by the division of many against one. That aesthetic structure changed, during the Occupation, into a political war of many against many that still holds true for *La Peste*. Because the plague is also internalized, that public war coexists with an inner conflict, one of varying intensity for each character, best described as one against one, a man against his private sickness, the god he wants to be.

As narrator and protagonist, Rieux sets the high, moral tone of the book and brings the other characters to life. Grand is able to talk to him as is true of all the characters who enter his sphere of influence. Through Rieux we meet and know everyone.

He inspires speech and that sense of physical presence that speech can give. Since Rieux, as narrator, tries to be scrupulously objective, the matters at hand are rendered faithfully. He is also the main character, intensely subjective while at the same time endowed with good will and compassion, co-requisite qualities that permit him to "recueillir les confidences" (TRN, 1222) and to transpose them into a book with a minimum of distortion. In his own estimation he is a witness. Rieux does not say nearly so much as the others in the novel. He listens. As narrator he says it all, even when he is quoting. Because Rieux is both narrator and protagonist his relationship with other characters is doubly significant. They were attracted to him and they came to him during a crisis as independent individuals. As a writer he is creating them out of the matrix of his own experience. We know that Camus considered this book both a personal confession and a report. Tarrou alone enjoys a similar relationship in his diary. His own interests, however, are focused on Rieux and Cottard, and we can understand how his desire for sanctity can partake both of base profiteering and selflessness, one trait refracted among three personalities. Rieux's journal, on the other hand, includes all the characters.

Rieux, like Camus, is an author, and Camus has set up between his representative and the other characters a system of parallel situations. This parallelism, like the similar statements made by Tarrou and Cottard concerning their previous experiences with pestilence, serves as an analytical device. Specific traits of one character are brought into relief by their echo in another. Since Camus is concerned with solidarity, similarities will be stressed, thereby making sacrifice and cooperation possible. Separate individuals gradually become a cohesive group and acquire another identity when they discover what they have in common. Rieux and Tarrou, for example, are both authors of a journal; Paneloux's first sermon on innate evil is taken up again, minus Christian terminology, in Tarrou's description of his past; Rieux's mother reminds Tarrou of his own, so much so that, when he moves in, he and Rieux become brothers; Grand, Rieux, and Rambert are separated from their wives. The number of these pairings is virtually infinite. As a result, each character, by a kind of stylistic intimacy, opens up into another and all of them join in Rieux. Just as Rieux's "I" is assimilated in the general "they," so does each individual, by an effect of reciprocity, illuminate the personality of Rieux. With each psychological revelation there is association, often a positive one, similar to Camus' discovery of other strangers.

At the same time, in keeping with the tragic vision of *La Peste*, the vision that transcends those circumstances that fall within the province of human legislation, we also realize that with each revelation there is complicity. That complicity arises from the fact that the plague is viewed not only as an invasion from outside but as a projection of evil from within. Those same parallel situations, be they metaphors, an entire scene, a profession, or turn of phrase, not only encourage a dynamic relationship between the characters, but allow Camus to give his attention first to the historical event and secondly to the psychological evil embodied by those same historically determined characters. The major characters confront the plague they each resemble. As we read on black passes over into white. Early in the book, when referring to the plague, Rieux admits: "Pour lutter contre l'abstraction, il faut un peu lui ressembler" (TRN, 1293). The plague is abstract because it kills impersonally and democratically, without reasons or distinctions. Rieux also deals in abstraction, in statistics and, as a doctor, he too does not become personally involved with his patients. He is of course assuming at this moment that he is adapting to a specific reality, that he is temporarily fighting an enemy with its own weapons, employing a kind of sympathetic medicine. Camus, however, soon makes us realize that the enemy is closer, that if the historical catalyst for writing *La Peste* was Nazism, the novel itself supplements a documentary with a tragic, nonhistorical vision in which the characters, through their own guilt, join their oppressors. *La Peste* is a historical novel because time passes, men act, and things change. It also focuses on ineradicable evil.

Tarrou's torment over what he was convinced was his murderous nature is resolved in his ideal role as "meurtrier innocent." His desire to deny that nature is presented to us as an extreme. The other characters do not deny but prefer to reconcile two powerful but contradictory impulses, to kill and to be innocent, contradictory until we realize that to kill is to be God and to be God is to be innocent.

If unable to kill directly, however, one can evolve a system. Paneloux's first sermon, for example, attempts to justify death by plague on the grounds of merited suffering: "Mes frères, vous êtes dans le malheur, mes frères, vous l'avez mérité" (TRN, 1296). Whatever empathy is expressed in "frères" dissolves quickly: "Paneloux se redressa alors, respira profondément" (TRN, 1296). The priest, high above his congregation, enjoys the pleasure of condemning, an "objective" condemnation since it translates God's will, as well as the pleasure of innocence, the absence of direct responsibility. Paneloux gradually becomes aware that God's objective will can serve subjective needs. Although tortured by doubt he will not deny God's existence. Referring to the death of children he concedes: "Il fallait la vouloir parce que Dieu la voulait" (TRN, 1403).

Paneloux's dilemma as a priest is a traditional one but Tarrou's accusation also applies to nonbelievers who do not have recourse to an external transcendental principle. Rambert's love for his absent wife, for example, reveals a more subtle and original variant of Tarrou's ideal: "Le grand désir d'un coeur inquiet est de posséder interminablement l'être qu'il aime ou de pouvoir plonger cet être, quand le temps de l'absence est venu, dans un sommeil sans rêves qui ne puisse prendre fin qu'au jour de la réunion" (TRN, 1307–8). Rambert is more than a spectator. He is not interpreting someone else's will but expressing his own. Out of overwhelming passion and possessiveness, he would like to kill the woman he loves, thus guaranteeing her fidelity, and he maintains his innocence by replacing her death with a dreamless sleep, a reality with a cliché! The resurrection of this sleeping beauty and female Lazarus would be accomplished by his return, and her life, like a text, would be bounded by his.

The majority of Camus' works are populated with characters who, for various reasons, kill or wish to kill innocently: Patrice Mersault who kills without remorse; Caligula the artist-emperor; Meursault who blames the sun; Jan's mother and sister in *Le Malentendu* who claim they are not killing their victims but merely advancing their inevitable death; the Resistants themselves who had to kill the enemy; and many of the characters in *La Peste* such as Paneloux, Rambert, Othon, Tarrou's father, Tarrou himself as revolutionary, and Rieux.

Camus makes Rieux a doctor in order to break the long chain of flamboyant heroes such as Caligula and, in *Le Mythe de Sisyphe*, the artist, the actor, Don Juan, and the conquerors. The doctor as principal character corresponds to Camus' new sense of commitment after the Liberation because he does not move on a stage but among equals and because his authority is professional, not miraculous or divine.

Rieux is extremely important to Camus because, having variously imagined his relationship to society as that of an emperor with slaves, a stranger persecuted, a hero saving victims, he is now seeking equality as well as a political purpose that would reflect a more normative view of human nature. Hence Rieux's status as doctor. The salvation that had been centered in the hero outside of or on the margins of society now has its locus in a more average man and his community. The society that was once a pretext has become the text, the true matter at hand. Camus now has doubts about saviors.

Unlike virtually all his predecessors, Rieux has a past, in this instance his mother. She is neither dead nor a murderess. Caring for her son, Madame Rieux is neither the indifferent figure Camus evoked in *L'Envers et l'endroit* nor the "devouring" mother in *Le Mythe de Sisyphe*. Like the former, however, she possesses an extraordinary presence and inspires the same intimate bond. She ministers to her son's pain and Doctor Rieux, ministering to the pain of others, embodies the vital continuity that can obtain between a parent and child. For these reasons Rieux is not heroic. Differing from Tarrou, he believes there is merit in being what he is, and what he is belongs as much to the past, his mother and his training, as it does to his independence.

Camus also makes him a doctor in order to investigate the mechanism by which a man can come to the aid of victims, all the while identifying, willingly or not, with the disease. Rieux puts the matter squarely: "Son rôle n'était plus de guérir. Son rôle était de diagnostiquer. Découvrir, voir, décrire, enregistrer, puis condamner, c'était sa tâche" (TRN, 1375). Rieux condemns and the distinction between killing and condemning is what distinguishes the guilty murderer from the innocent murderer who is a murderer once removed. Insofar as he is a doctor he is obliged to accept what is inevitable. To paraphrase Paneloux, he has to want it because the plague wants it. In *L'Etat de siège* Camus will create the character of the Secretary who, pen and paper in hand, follows the Plague as he makes his rounds. The central ambiguity of the novel, however, lies in the extent to which Rieux accepts Tarrou's pessimistic analysis of the murderous human heart. Such psychological pessimism ordinarily justifies a repressive society to keep it in check, such as the one we have before us in *La Peste*. Tarrou then becomes an accomplice. Complete optimism regarding human nature requires minimal government in order to allow for the unimpeded expressions of innocence and goodness. But Rieux is no fool. He

gives Tarrou's views his undivided attention and Tarrou becomes his soul-brother. To what extent, we then ask, are Rieux
the protagonist and Rieux the narrator one and the same man?
How far is the distance from Rieux to Camus on this question of
plague? We note that the plague goes beyond Rieux's profession to include his personal life, beyond what is inevitable to what is
avoidable. Rambert's fantasy about his wife's dreamless sleep is
echoed, for example, in Rieux's description of his mother:

> Le docteur regardait . . . sa mère, sagement assise dans un coin de la
> salle à manger, sur une chaise. . . . Elle attendait. . . . Quelque chose
> changeait dans le visage de sa mère lorsqu'il apparaissait. Tout ce
> qu'une vie laborieuse y avait mis de mutisme semblait s'animer alors.
> Puis, elle retombait dans le silence. (TRN, 1389)

Rieux arrives and his mother comes to life; he leaves and she
falls silent, which in the novel's own terms is the equivalent of
death.[13] Rieux also transfers to his own mother vocabulary previously used by Paneloux to describe the plague: "Voyez-le, cet
ange de la peste, beau comme Lucifer et brillant comme le mal
lui-même. . . . La peste entre chez vous, s'assied dans votre
chambre et attend votre retour. Elle est là, patiente et attentive,
assurée comme l'ordre même du monde" (TRN, 1297). By this
association of imagery, Camus is describing two mothers, one
the giver of life, the other, like Mother Earth, its recipient. Paneloux's description splits the monolithic nature of the plague
into two persons, the male angel of evil and the goddess of
death, the one who enters, the one who waits. The dualism ex-
tends to Rieux, a doctor making his visits whom the citizens
gradually identify as death's messenger. He comes to certify
what is already there.

Rieux's mother is not the plague but together they embody
one very important aspect of the plague. They are living together because Rieux has sent his wife to a sanitarium. The entire novel grows out of this incident which coincides with the
first signs of the epidemic.

13. TRN, 1392–98.

Rieux has what Jan in *Le Malentendu* wished for. Tarrou's definition of the plague was single and absolute, and he presented it emphatically and with absolutely no discussion. Rieux, in contrast, describes many events which, by their contiguity, suggest several interpretations. It is also Rieux who enriches the narrative with references to the past plagues of history. The only one that he does not mention directly is the plague of sterility caused by the incestuous marriage of Oedipus to his mother Jocasta, the one which is relevant to his personal life and which has nothing to do with history.

Except for the mother, there is in *La Peste* an almost total absence of female characters, particularly wives. Describing the Bowery during his visit to New York after the war, Camus had written: "C'est le quartier le plus sinistre de la ville, celui où l'on ne rencontre pas une femme" (C, 2, 50). The fraternity of Rieux, Rambert, Grand, Paneloux, and Tarrou, all of them celibate, through choice or circumstance, has, like the plague, created its desert. Madame Rieux has been replaced by Madame Rieux and Rieux, who cried when Tarrou died, orders his mother not to cry when he learns of the death of his wife. If tears symbolize loss, then no one has been lost. If they are the visible evidence of remorse, there is none. Meursault sent away his mother, Rieux his wife. *La Peste* ends where *L'Etranger* began, with a telegram announcing a death. Camus analyzes not only the reaction (or lack of a reaction) to a death but its cause. Rieux asked his wife's forgiveness for having neglected to take proper care of her. The plague amplifies that neglect and transforms it from an unfortunate result of unforeseeable circumstances, which is true, into a covert act of aggression, which is also true. A wife is replaced by a mother and there are no other women left. The plague, therefore, is both the cause and the result of separation. It is suffered and desired, both history and psychology. The sterility that reigns in Oran is the *sine qua non* of exiled wives and celibate men. Camus announced this theme in an editorial:

La France a vécu beaucoup de tragédies qui, aujourd'hui, ont reçu leur dénouement. Elle en vivra encore beaucoup d'autres qui n'ont pas commencé. Mais il en est une que, depuis cinq ans, les hommes et les femmes de ce pays n'ont pas cessé de souffrir, c'est celle de la séparation. , . .

Il y a cinq ans que des Français et des Françaises attendent. Il y a cinq ans que dans leur coeur sevré, ils luttent désespérément contre le temps, contre l'idée que l'absence vieillit et que toutes ces années sont perdues pour l'amour et le bonheur. (E, 299)

The male solidarity whose outlines Camus sketched in *Le Mythe de Sisyphe*, whose courageous self-sacrifice he personally witnessed in the Resistance, and whose virtue he extolled in *Combat*, represented sanity, an antidote to the imperial vision. It never ceases to be that but Camus, for the first time, turns male solidarity around and reveals that the sterility he had praised in *Le Mythe de Sisyphe* as the ultimate virtue is also the plague.

Camus' long and detailed description of the death of Judge Othon's child, in a chapter which, after many readings, remains unbearable, vividly portrays the human consequences of an idealized sterility.[14] His death is witnessed by all concerned, Rieux, Tarrou, Rambert, and Paneloux. They can do nothing. Are they therefore nothing more than witnesses, objective spectators at someone else's crucifixion? Does their anguish at what they are seeing register only their failure to cure or are there other factors to consider? What precisely is the relationship between saviors and victims? One answer can be found in a series of related images deployed throughout the novel which inform the reader what the child's death ultimately means to Camus:

Les flammes de la peste dévoraient leur tribut chaque soir. (TRN, 1364)

Les feux de joie de la peste brûlaient avec une allégresse toujours plus grande dans le four crématoire. (TRN, 1412)

Ils niaient . . . que nous ayons été ce peuple abasourdi dont tous les jours une partie, entassée dans la gueule d'un four, s'évaporait en fumées grasses. (TRN, 1465)

14. Stepan, the most radical member of the group of revolutionnaries in *Les Justes* states: "Quand nous nous déciderons à oublier les enfants, ce jour-là, nous serons les maîtres du monde et la révolution triomphera" (TRN, 336).

Insofar as the victims include all the citizens of Oran, men, women, and children, Camus is reminding the reader of· the Nazi concentration camps and the ovens used to burn Jews. The plague is also visualized as Moloch, whose rituals specifically required the sacrifice of children thrown into the open, burning stomach of a statue. Evoked by Rieux, his presence dissolves the middle ground of humanity and transforms all the victims into children. We also have a specific child's death witnessed by Rieux and all the major characters. Moloch, or Baal, was the god of fertility, which fact conferred transcendental purpose and therefore innocence upon both the god and the practitioners of infanticide. For Camus, the death of children reverses the process of procreation and time moves backward to sterility. That sterility occurs when, in a reversal of the usual chronology, wives are replaced by mothers and husbands become sons. The banding together of these sons in a fraternity of bachelors leaves no room for children. Camus' wife gave birth to twins in 1945. The description of the child's death, the book's central episode, was written by a man who, with the exception of his own dangerous illness, had never before been so vulnerable. That vulnerability, the price for living one's life through others and therefore risking it, makes Rieux's grief real. The plague, therefore, is not in the multiple roles and responsibilities we assume in life, it is in the single, exclusive role that reduces the complex and contradictory dimensions of a personality to a celibate abstraction. In the novel, Rieux is either a son *or* a husband, seldom both at the same time. Something in Rieux evidently responds to that kind of simplicity, or rather, oversimplification, and the child's death reminds him of the price they are both paying.[15]

L'Etranger opposed an innocent man to his executioners. In *Le Mythe de Sisyphe* innocent heroes came to the aid of innocent victims. The heroes now are inhabited by plague. There has certainly been a transformation but not all that much has changed. Absolutely innocent or absolutely evil the heart is still simple, and the simple heart, Camus said, in alliance with genius, would

15. Thomas Merton, *Albert Camus's The Plague* (New York: Seabury Press, 1968), p. 12.

revolutionize society. It would indeed! The murdered innocence whose cry Camus heard in *Promethée aux enfers*, an analysis
of why he joined the resistance, is amplified in *La Peste* by the
dying child's last howl of pain. The serum the doctors admin-
istered to save his life increased his resistance and only pro-
longed his agony. What Camus hears now is that innocence, to
remain innocent, must be murdered. The child must die to save
his savior, Rieux, to save his idea or image of innocence. He becomes the evidence every idea needs to survive, dead evidence,
not the kind that is alive and evolving, requiring perpetual
reassessments.

By the same token, a wife must be absént, asleep, or dead to
be loved. Camus devotes many chapters to the depiction of separated lovers desperately trying to communicate with each other
through any means at their disposal. This exile, which Camus
had experienced during the Occupation when he had only recently remarried, is transposed into the book, and his description of loneliness and desire can be included among some of the
most moving and profound pages he has ever written. The misogynist passages in the *Carnets* have not disappeared but Camus, in 1944, offers an important revision:

> Ceux qui aiment toutes les femmes sont ceux qui sont en route vers
> l'abstraction. Ils dépassent ce monde, quoiqu'il y paraisse. Car ils se dé-
> tournent du particulier, du cas singulier. L'homme qui fuirait toute idée
> et toute abstraction, le vrai désesperé, est l'homme d'une seule femme.
> Par entêtement dans ce visage singulier qui ne peut satisfaire à tout. (C,
> 2, 126)

Camus is taking a critical look at his chapter on Don Juan which
he ostensibly composed as an ode to the body and to sensual
love. Love concentrated in one beloved was tantamount to folly,
an abstraction of the body's infinite incarnations. Now "quantity" is equated with superficiality, a new synonym for abstraction. Rieux has one wife. Camus is reversing the terms he used
in *Le Mythe de Sisyphe* but only to seek out a balance between self-
absorption and dispersion. He also knows that as long as the self
is imperial, its own transcendental principle, it will continue to
derive its fullest satisfactions from others who exist but who

must, in one form or another, be absent. The chapters on love in *La Peste* are deeply felt but no one is there. Camus, as an author, is inspired by absence and its inevitable companion, the doctrine of self-sufficiency. It is absence that provides the connection between the plague, creator of dead or absent people, the speeches of Grand and Rambert inspired by absent wives, the child who has to die to be innocent and to be loved, and the fraternity of saviours who will save humanity provided it is dehumanized. Because of absence, image takes precedence over reality, and what started as commitment ends up again as a mirror. The separation of lovers and the death of children are the banal facts of history. But when there is consent and complicity, then history passes over into ethics.

La Peste is a unique work in the corpus of Camus' fiction because it alone, in the persons of Tarrou and Rieux, embodies Camus' past as well as the future direction of his work. Tarrou wants to be an innocent murderer, a saint without God, in other words God himself. Of all the characters, he is the most heroic and Camus puts him here because the rejection of the past is no longer the cherished doctrine it used to be, because he is pessimistic though not absolutely, and because the emphasis is henceforth on evolution, not revolution.

The figure of Tarrou is still close to Camus and, to this extent, Rieux and Tarrou represent opposite yet correlated ends of a moral spectrum ranging from altruistic self-denial to egotistical heroism. Camus is ethically and aesthetically diversifying his own sense of himself. Not all the figures in this spectrum, however, are equal.

Rieux wants to be a man and it is Rieux who is the main character and author of this chronicle. He too embodies an imperial vision but not completely and with a more critical spirit than his friend. Tarrou is so lucid he is blind to everything except what his lucidity is fixed on. Rieux, who can be distracted, moves with a more complicated, less systematic humanity which in itself is medicine to the single-minded purpose of the plague. The child's death condemns something in Rieux, but not everything. Rieux's private plague, his relationship to his mother, does not exhaust the meanings he has for us. He speaks for love and solidarity, and puts his hand on the dying child's wrist hoping, by some miracle, to give him his own life; at the same time, in his private life and in his profession, he creates and lives in his own desert and his own sterility. Because the other characters are not so lucid as Tarrou, (even Paneloux doubts,) their very uncertainty or indecisiveness which can propel them into a holocaust can also bring them back again. Whereas Rieux is aware that he resembles the plague, he goes only so far as simile whereas Tarrou goes all the way to metaphor and joins indissolubly what Rieux brings together for the purposes of analysis. Of the entire group consisting of Rieux, Tarrou, Rambert, Paneloux, and Grand, it is Paneloux and Tarrou who die. They were the absolutists. They were not killed by the plague which filled them entirely. The plague left and they became nothing. In contrast to the other characters, they had, each in his own way, institutionalized the plague, in the case of Tarrou, by excluding everything else from human nature, in the case of Paneloux, by representing a specific church doctrine. Camus identified this doctrine in 1944: "Le christianisme dans son essence . . . est une doctrine de l'injustice. Il est fondé sur le sacrifice de l'innocent et l'acceptation de ce sacrifice" (E, 271). In more personal terms, Camus knew that one did not have to be a Christian to institutionalize killing:

Ce n'est pas me réfuter en effet que de réfuter la non-violence. Je n'ai jamais plaidé pour elle. . . . Je crois que la violence est inévitable, les années d'occupation me l'ont appris. Pour tout dire, il y a eu, en ce temps-là, de terribles violences qui ne m'ont posé aucun problème. . . . Je dis seulement qu'il faut refuser toute légitimation de la violence, que cette légitimation lui vienne d'une raison d'Etat absolue, ou d'une philosophie totalitaire. La violence est à la fois inévitable et injustifiable. Je crois qu'il faut lui garder son caractère exceptionnel et la resserrer dans les limites qu'on peut. (E, 355)

Systematic violence or nonviolence, the demonic or the saintly, become two faces of God which Camus rejects, though not equally, in favor of a more complex and unpredictable human nature. As a result, Rieux never acts with his total self at any one given moment. The institutions of violence would echo an institutionalized psychology, a self absolutely independent because secure in its own self-knowledge. When, on the other hand, there is contradiction, and contradiction is not a monologue but, literally, an inner dialogue, then affirmations are replaced by approximations and a community that embodies it.

If Doctor Rieux is keenly aware of human contact and of the necessity for objective distance, aware also that he can both cure and condemn, he also knows, as does Camus, that he too, as a writer, must participate and keep his distance, to engage in experience and withdraw from it. Tarrou's view is that he runs the risk of killing. Rieux, who agrees, would add that he also runs the risk of saving. As in the phrase, "s'oublier à moitié," balance is all. Years later, he told his audience in Stockholm: "L'artiste se forge dans cet aller-retour perpétuel de lui aux autres" (E, 1072).

Tarrou is also an author and he too takes considerable risks as he moves about in society. In his pursuit of moral superiority, he does not succumb to Romantic evasions or fantasize, like Valéry in "Palme," about his self-fecundating powers, although traces of such attitudes can be detected in his claim to omniscience. He joins and organizes the community and, through his writings, tries to keep his distance. He fails. Rieux attributes the encroaching anarchy in Tarrou's journal to his failure to maintain objectivity. Tarrou has abolished the distance that separates him from others and he becomes infected. Paradoxically, that same subjectivity which would have ordinarily enhanced the human qualities of another character destroy Tarrou because of the distance he falls from his divine nature as he believes it to be or as he believes it should be. He loses control of himself, thereby abdicating his authorship, his authority and all claims to the throne, like a careless prince or the brother who did not make it. He told Rieux that men who are distracted risk killing, and it is precisely when Rieux is distracted, his eyes blinded by tears while trying to save Tarrou's life, that Tarrou succumbs. Meursault too is blinded, but Rieux is not responsible in any way for Tarrou's death and there is no trial.

Rieux survives because he is not only a doctor but an author who succeeded in establishing the proper rhythm between subjective participation and objective distance, solidarity and self-interest. Each one, in its extreme form, in the absence of its antithesis, becomes the plague. Camus' awareness of antithesis and contradiction no longer produces heroes endeavoring desperately to overcome them. Now those contradictions will be multiplied. The new style will be proof of the man.

Rieux also survives because the instinct to kill is not altogether condemned. Occupying the middle ground of humanity, he is aware that accidental or unpremeditated violence falls within the generally accepted limits of human behavior.[16] The plague is totalitarian and can inhabit the individual as much as the state. Tarrou would eliminate the slightest trace of aggression and substitutes for the institution of violence the institution of grace. As for Camus, overcoming repeated attacks of tuberculosis and ill health in 1930, 1937, and 1942 and having gone through the Occupation, that other plague, he knew that if he was to fight being killed, by others or by himself, it would help to have the killer instinct. He would abandon the simple heart, absolutely good or absolutely evil, on the grounds it was not human.

La Peste enjoyed almost unanimous praise when it was published. It was, after all, fiction. When Camus wrote *L'Homme révolté*, however, he caused a scandal among the saints and among a few devils too.

16. After the publication of *La Peste*, Camus wrote in his notebooks: "Revaloriser le meurtre pour l'opposer à la destruction anonyme et froide, et abstraite" (C, 2, 275).

4 / From Revolution to Rebellion

BORN of a mother, hence burdened with a past, the imperial self, like ancient heroes, seeks new parents, gods usually, who define not so much where he came from but that glory to which he aspires. Caligula the emperor, Meursault the stranger, Don Juan and the other conquerors of *Le Mythe*, the fraternity of *La Peste*, are so many divine identities, singular and plural, that Camus will assume and then, gradually, reject. Rieux's claim, when confronted with Tarrou's sanctity, that he desires solely to be a man reminds us again of that other and important part of Camus, the debunking satirist able and willing to gain purchase into the human community and to confront himself.

In 1944, Camus had written in separate editorials: "Il s'agit de faire le salut de l'homme" (E, 179) and "Il n'y a pas de mérite à être ce qu'on est" (E, 1544). The same reforming and radical spirit applies to both statements because human nature, in its concrete political or psychological expressions, in what it owes to the past, its own or the history of institutions, is overlooked in favor of a new man and a new society. According to Roger

Quilliot, Camus had private reservations about what he was saying in his editorials regarding revolutionary politics and, by extension, revolutionary psychology. His letters to the poet Francis Ponge inform us that, as early as 1943, Camus attempted to introduce a keener sense of relativity and psychological realism into the abstract affirmations of his communist friend concerning the future of society.[1] At the same time, the writing of *La Peste*, where the heroes themselves are, in part, the plague, the spread of Stalinist communism, and Camus' own self-analysis, more and more forced those private feelings into the open. In a series of texts written between 1945 and 1948, among them "Remarque sur la révolte" (E, 1682–1697) and "Ni victimes ni bourreaux" (E, 329–352),[2] both an attack on Stalinism, a speech, "L'Incroyant et les chrétiens," (E, 367–375), given at the monastery of Latour-Maubourg, another entitled "Le Témoin de la liberté" (E, 397–406), and in his essay "L'Exil d'Hélène" (E, 851–57),[3] Camus will alter, if not negate entirely, the absolutism of those two statements. He now informs the Dominican monks: "Il n'y a donc de dialogue possible qu'entre des gens qui restent ce qu'ils sont et qui parlent vrai" (E, 372). In *Le Mythe*, Camus had offered the following view as the fundamental axiom of a radical psychology: "Il n'y a pas de frontière entre ce qu'un homme veut être et ce qu'il est" (E, 159). At that point in his life, will power took precedence over reality. Now Camus admits the need less to change himself than, having called, so to speak, for time out, to know himself. In his polemic with Emmanuel d'Astier de la Vigerie who had attacked "Ni victimes ni bourreaux" along traditional Communist lines,[4] Camus summarizes a more conservative view of himself and his place in society: "Mon rôle, je le reconnais, n'est pas de transformer le monde, ni l'homme; je n'ai pas assez de vertus, ni de lumières pour cela. Mais il est, peut-être, de servir, à ma place, les quelques valeurs sans lesquelles un monde, même transformé, ne vaut pas la peine d'être

---

1. Quilliot quotes several brief passages from the correspondence, (E, 1566).
2. "Remarque" was incorporated into *L'Homme révolté*.
3. "L'Exil d'Hélène" was republished in 1954 in *L'Eté*, a collection of lyrical essays Camus had written between 1939 and 1953.
4. D'Astier de la Vigerie wrote two articles: "Arrachez la victime aux bourreaux" and "Ponce Pilate chez les bourreaux."

vécu, sans lesquelles un homme, même nouveau, ne vaudra pas d'être respecté" (E, 368). Camus evidently considers these as yet unspecified values to be permanent, therefore rooted in the past and appropriate as moral guidelines. Consequently, he gives the impression less of moving inexorably toward Utopia than standing still in a vortex. Political ideology, oriented towards the future and, to that extent, prone to abstract syntheses, is coming to terms with psychology, with a human and limited self that is what it is whatever it does. At this point in his life Camus is much less interested in a projected image of himself than in an introspective, analytical, and ultimately pragmatic style of life. He writes in "L'Exil d'Hélène": "Nous allumons dans un ciel ivre les soleils que nous voulons. Mais il n'empêche que les bornes existent et que nous le savons" (E, 854). False suns, false selves, and false politics, Camus would denounce all three in *L'Homme révolté*.

The impulse that inspires a man to be a god, an impulse Camus calls an inherent "appetite" (E, 555),[5] is one of three factors responsible for revolt. A crisis is triggered because one of the goals of revolt is to remove whatever thwarts its trajectory towards absolute freedom and omnipotence. Since revolt, creating or responding to violence, often leads to killing, it must eventually come to terms with the notions of guilt and innocence. Such moral concerns, at first, seem hardly essential: "Qu'est-ce qu'être un Dieu. Reconnaître justement que tout est permis; refuser toute autre loi que la sienne propre. . . . Devenir Dieu, c'est accepter le crime" (E, 648). The acute awareness of the relativity of customs and laws and their moral equivalency, implicit in the phrase "tout est permis," has apparently fostered neither political nor personal modesty but an unbridled will to power. Since the French Revolution, the gradual abolition in Europe of all political and moral institutions which had once enjoyed the status of intrinsic merit and which were designed, in theory, to support the members of society, threw

---

5. "Rien ne peut décourager l'appétit de divinité au coeur de l'homme. D'autres sont venus et viennent qui, oubliant Waterloo, prétendent toujours terminer l'histoire. La divinité de l'homme est encore en marche" (E, 555).

the individual back upon himself. There was nothing else. Anarchy replaced hierarchy. Camus' analyses of Romanticism and Surrealism develop as their central thesis the divinisation of the individual as a response to a moral and political vacuum.[6] While composing *l'Homme révolté*, Camus assigned this observation to his private notebooks: "La seule vocation que je me sente, c'est dire aux consciences qu'elles ne sont pas sans tache" (C, 2, 275). We can speculate that Camus put aside his manuscript of *La Mort heureuse* not only because it was, by his standards, poorly written but because its hero Patrice Meursault, guilty of premeditated murder, remains throughout the novel a lucid and amoral criminal. Such a hero embodied an intolerable contradiction. How can one "know" and not be troubled? If not morally unacceptable, such a character was at least boring aesthetically. Camus created in his place Meursault who commits crimes passively, without knowledge. He is condemned, but by others, and he is innocent as long as his life remains unexamined. Referring to the American novel of the thirties and forties, to the "hard" school of writing that influenced *L'Etranger*,[7] Camus set up an equation between "innocence" and purely physiological description, that is to say, "appearance":

Le roman américain . . . refuse l'analyse, la recherche d'un ressort psychologique fondamental qui expliquerait et résumerait la conduite d'un personnage. . . . Sa technique consiste à décrire les hommes par l'extérieur, . . . à faire enfin comme si les hommes se définissaient entièrement par leurs automatismes quotidiens. . . . On s'explique ainsi le nombre considérable "d'innocents" utilisés dans cet univers. L'innocent est le sujet idéal d'une telle entreprise puisqu'il n'est défini, et tout entier, que par son comportement. (E, 668–69)

Defining ourselves by our bearing alone was to assign our identity to the present and to exclude any consideration either of the past or of memory. Meursault, however, does commit crimes. In

---

6. We may note another vacuum, the absence of a father; like two of their predecessors, Robespierre and Saint-Just, three twentieth-century "conquerors," Malraux, Sartre, and Camus were brought up by their mothers.

7. Camus is thinking of Hemingway, Steinbeck, and even Faulkner.

Camus' novel, therefore, it was not the character that inspired the style, but the style itself adopted by Meursault to tell his own story that created innocence. Camus himself joined the Resistance because he had heard "le cri de l'innocence assassinée" (E, 842). That innocence, that apparently verifiable fact would pass over to him and justify whatever acts he and his "brothers" had to perform in the service of humanity. *La Peste* questioned these assumptions because it reinstated the inner life. Consequently, Camus had to modify his notions of guilt and innocence at the very least in the direction of greater psychological complexity. He had once compared his enrollment in the Resistance to a descent into hell. Unlike Dante, however, he also proclaimed: "Pour toujours je serai étranger à moi-même" (E, 111), and he thought he would make his journey unscathed by introspection. He would be the chronicler of hell, not its resident. When Rieux, who doubts his own virtue, puts his hand on the dying child's wrist, it is not only to transfer his life to a victim, but also in the hope that the child's Christlike innocence would pass over to him. They are both dying, though in different ways. There is plague. The child dies and it is evil, no longer an alien force, that enters the hero. Although that evil still possesses a demonic and therefore divine intensity, Camus, increasingly interested in flaws, motives, and human subterfuge, is moving in the direction of a normative, analytical morality:

L'homme est la seule créature qui refuse d'être ce qu'elle est. La question est de savoir si ce refus ne peut l'amener qu'à la destruction des autres et de lui-même, si toute révolte doit s'achever en justification du meurtre universel, ou si, au contraire, sans prétention à une impossible innocence, elle peut découvrir le principe d'une culpabilité raisonnable. (E, 420)

Since at least 1945 Camus was anxious publicly to modify the blunt, almost Manichean opposition between good and evil, innocence and guilt that had provided the foundation of so much of his thinking. "Impossible innocence" and "culpabilité raisonnable" represent options in favor of approximate ethics. Those same options underscore another significant change. Immediately after the Liberation Camus, in his capacity as newspaper editor, demanded the death penalty for certain collaborationists such as Pucheu, engaging himself meanwhile in a debate with François Mauriac who was arguing for Christian compassion. Camus' language at this time reveals a side of his character not well known to the general public: "Qui oserait parler ici du pardon?" (E, 259); "Nous savons aujourd'hui que l'ennemi doit être exterminé" (E, 1544); "Il faut . . . songer à punir. Et cet horrible mot a toujours répugné à des coeurs un peu délicats. Il a fallu pourtant nous faire à cette idée, prendre en charge la justice humaine, accepter de trancher ce qui était à trancher" (E, 1548–49); "Il fallait . . . accepter résolument de paraître injustes pour servir réellement la justice" (E, 1549); "Un pays qui manque son épuration se prépare à manquer sa rénovation" (E, 1550).[8] Camus appears to have held certain truths, particularly the notion of justice, to be self-evident. In fact, he was never really that sure either of himself or of justice. In 1946 he told his audience at the monastery: "Ne me sentant en possession d'aucune vérité absolue et d'aucun message . . . j'en suis venu à reconnaître en moi-même, et publiquement ici que . . . François Mauriac avait raison contre moi" (E, 371–72).[9]

The issue in *L'Homme révolté* is, of course, not punishment but capital punishment. Because Camus is increasingly interested in motives, the distinction between apparent injustice and "real" justice, between unalloyed portions of guilt and innocence are no longer valid. Marxism he defines and condemns as "une doctrine de culpabilité quant à l'homme, d'innocence quant à l'histoire" (E, 644); surrealist antitheism "s'affermit . . . sur une idée

---

8. In *L'Homme révolté*, Camus makes the following comments on the style of Saint-Just, prominent leader of the French Revolution: "Cette cascade d'affirmations péremptoires, ce style axiomatique et sentencieux, le peignent mieux que les portraits les plus fidèles. Les sentences ronronnent, comme la sagesse même de la nation, les définitions, qui font la science, se succèdent comme des commandements froids et clairs. 'Les principés doivent être modérés, les lois implacables, les peines sans retour.' C'est le style guillotine" (E, 533–34). Reading some of his own editorials in *Combat*, Camus also may have been judging himself.

9. Camus was anxious to declare publicly that he had changed his mind in order to demonstrate his allegiance to relative as opposed to absolute truths and to dialogue as the vehicle for change. Calling his polemic with Mauriac a dialogue, however, was perhaps straining definitions.

de la nonculpabilité absolue de l'homme" (E, 501); and the political rebel who kills or terrorizes "ne peut pas se sentir innocent. Il lui faut donc créer la culpabilité chez la victime" (E, 589). Camus is not interested, for example, in the opposing views of Marxists and surrealists regarding innocence or guilt but in their agreement on absolute distinctions. These distinctions in . turn confer dictatorial powers of justice to self-elected individuals. The issue of capital punishment had already caused considerable friction between Camus and Sartre who approved of it.

According to Eric Werner in *De la violence au totalitarisme*,[10] the issue of capital punishment was only one part of a much larger debate that captured the full attention of French intellectuals throughout the fifties: the justification of violence in all of its forms, particularly acts of political terrorism. Those on the left of the political spectrum, such as Simone de Beauvoir, Merleau-Ponty, Sartre, and Camus had no trouble condemning Fascist repression in Germany and Spain because Fascism was, in their view, totally irrational, a raw play for absolute power. The Stalin purges, however, and the reports of concentration camps throughout Russia and Eastern Europe in the fifties posed the problem of Communist violence. Sartre's basic contention, shared by Simone de Beauvoir and Merleau-Ponty, was that Communist violence, while regrettable, was justified because it was rational. The goal of Communism, spelled out clearly by Marx and his interpreters, was the establishment of the proletariat as sole ruler of the State and the emancipation of mankind through a classless society. Violent means justified the removal of human obstacles to the fulfillment of this objective, historical goal. Camus' concern, however, was not that certain means may or may not justify certain ends but, as he phrases it, "who" justified the means. The issue, therefore, was not the philosophical distinctions between rational or irrational violence but human nature and its ingrained appetite for domination. "Who" turns the debate into an investigation of psychological motives. Rejecting Sartre's "distinguo," Camus assimilates Fascism and Communism under the banner of nihilism.

The act of killing, in Camus' view, is what turns men into gods

10. De la violence au totalitarisme (Paris: Colemann-Lévy, 1972).

because the act replaces relative ethics with absolute guilt in the defendant and absolute innocence in the judge. Such rebels as Marx, Saint-Just, and Lenin are viewed not only as embodiments of some of the major developments in Western history but as *dramatis personae* in a unique tragedy, one in which Camus considered himself implicated, the creation of a race of innocent and murderous gods. Paying special attention to Saint-Just, prosecuting attorney in the trial of Louis XVI, Camus takes his famous accusation, "Nul ne peut régner innocemment" and changes it into "Nul n'est vertueux innocemment" (E, 532). That mischievous transformation was directed not only against Saint-Just, model of implacable virtue, but against himself. In his speech "Le Témoin de la liberté," Camus had already commented on the artist's virtue: "Nous sommes par nature les ennemis des idoles abstraites. . . . Non pas au nom de la morale et de la vertu. . . . Nous ne sommes pas des vertueux" (E, 405). Virtue is increasingly regarded by Camus less as a definitive summary of himself, or of any man, and more of an artifice, a public image designed to let vice pass, like Musset's Lorenzaccio only turned inside out, firstly because the cloak is a cloak of virtue, secondly because it is falling off.[11]

When he was editor of *Combat*, Camus was often referred to as a twentieth-century Saint-Just;[12] early in *La Peste* Rambert compares Rieux to Saint-Just;[13] and in 1949 Camus wrote the play *Les Justes* where, inspired by an early group of Russian terrorists, he attempts to formulate a political ethic that would require the life of the assassin in return for each assassination. Such an ethic, he hoped, would fully allow terrorism to fall within the precincts of the human. The play's title refers, apparently for the sake of contrast, to the Revolutionary leader who, though himself guillotined, never made any such equitable sacrifice. After the publication of *La Peste* in 1947 Camus acquired the reputation of a lay-saint, the embodiment of justice. One year

11. "Le vice a été pour moi un vêtement, maintenant il est collé à ma peau." *Lorenzaccio*, Act III, Scene iii.

12. Emmett Parker refers to the relationship between Camus' journalism and the figure of Saint-Just in *Albert Camus—The Artist in the Arena* (Madison and Milwaukee: University of Wisconsin Press, 1965), pp. 67, 82.

13. TRN, 1226–27.

later, aware of his own complicity in the creation of such a reputation, particularly through Tarrou, Camus made his public comment on the so-called virtuous artist. Also in the essay, "L'Enigme," written in 1950, Camus refers to his reputation for "austerity" and comments: "Je porte en effet le poids de cette réputation qui fait bien rire mes amis" (E, 863). The name Saint-Just itself was to become almost surreal in its application to Camus, a demonic pun. *L'Homme révolté* was one in a series of exorcisms. In an open letter written after its publication, Camus puts the matter squarely:

Si *L'Homme révolté* juge quelqu'un, c'est d'abord son auteur. Tous ceux pour qui les problèmes agités dans ce livre ne sont pas seulement rhétorique ont compris que j'analysais une contradiction qui avait été d'abord la mienne. . . . Je ne sais parler que de ce que j'ai vécu. J'ai vécu le nihilisme, la contradiction, la violence et le vertige de la destruction. . . . Mais je garde le droit de dire ce que je sais désormais sur moi et sur les autres. (E, 753)

L'Homme révolté examines the spirit of revolt from the French to the Russian Revolution, from the Marquis de Sade to the Surrealists, with extended analyses of Hegel, Marx, Nietzsche, the Romantics, Lautréamont, and Rimbaud. These historical figures and movements interest Camus because each one, to a different degree, embodies the second factor in revolt, the call for personal and political freedom.

Revolt, turning around and against oppression, posed special problems for Camus. The relationship with his mother described in the opening pages of the *Carnets* is based on the notion of a son's growing independence and the betrayal of his mother, one seemingly the inevitable sequel to the other.[14] The style of *Le Mythe de Sisyphe*, as Camus, ready to leave Algeria, looked back on his past, the landscapes of North Africa, and a mother's love, aggravated those two terms into a confrontation of hate. The "devouring" love that Camus evoked justified his portrayal of the parent as oppressor who in turn, being first, became the paradigm of all forms of oppression. Such a mother,

14. See pp. 12–13.

however, conflicted with his earlier portrait of an indifferent and passive woman who had never told her son that she loved him. From all evidence, the earlier portrait seems the more accurate one. The new man, nevertheless, made his break and was reborn. That betrayal was much more than inevitable. It was espoused and erected into a doctrine of total freedom.

As if he were now aware, not of his ambivalent feelings toward his mother, but of the brutal manner in which he used those feelings, Camus sets himself the difficult task of redefining revolt in terms of both liberation and reconciliation, in terms of what he owes to himself and to others. It was the issue of reconciliation that separated him from his historical predecessors and, eventually, from such contemporary peers as Merleau-Ponty and Jean-Paul Sartre.[15] A member once of the Communist party, an active Resistant, Camus, nevertheless, by 1945, was becoming less and less the revolutionary. His personal and political revolt had been based on ignorance of motives and on the radical assumption that each "act" or decision was devoid of psychological causality. The change in Camus is due in part to the transfer of his attention from Nazism to Communism. Less certain of himself because he had once been a Communist, more and more introspective, it is becoming essential for Camus that revolt constitute not a break but a continuity, that revolt measure its validity not against abstract political theory but against his own self-analysis and perceptions of human psychology. In a footnote Camus writes: "Toute idéologie se constitue contre la psychologie" (E, 525). L'Homme révolté is an attempt to reverse that process.

Camus' critique of the historical figures from the French Rev-

---

15. Camus considered Merleau-Ponty's *Humanisme et terreur* an apology for terrorism and, after a bitter quarrel with the author one evening at the home of Boris Vian, broke off relations. The extremely critical analyses of *L'Homme révolté* that appeared in Jean-Paul Sartre's journal *Les Temps modernes* were responsible for the final break-up of a friendship that had already shown signs of strain. First appeared Francis Jeanson's review in May, 1952, entitled "Albert Camus ou l'âme révoltée." Camus' response (E, 754–74), directed against both Jeanson and Sartre, appeared in *Les Temps modernes* in August of the same year together with a rejoinder by Sartre, later published in *Situations 4*, and a second article by Jeanson, "Pour tout vous dire."

olution to the present contends that the rebel, by opposing his oppressor, be it the King or the Church, parent, master, or superior social class, legitimately demands his freedom and the liberation of his fellowman; however, by killing his oppressor, he succeeds only in taking his place. Camus calls this unholy succession: "Tuer Dieu et bâtir une église" (E, 510). The rebel, by murdering, becomes a revolutionary or antirebel. As if by a primitive psychological process, by a mechanism of guilt and compensation (or atonement), he assumes the identity of his victim and denies that the murder ever took place. This transferal of identity guarantees succession and constitutes a reversal of the rebel's initial intent, which was liberation, and the tragic realization of his own will to power.

Camus does agree with the first principle of revolt: "Pour être, l'homme doit se révolter" (E, 431). This "existence" is not biological birth but the necessary rite of passage into manhood. Self-affirmation, however, must lead to the discovery of people because that same affirmation, in the absence of resistance, of other lives, would either dissolve or, if unchecked, become oppressive. Through this discovery the outlines of a human community begin to emerge: "Chacun dit à l'autre qu'il n'est pas Dieu" (E, 709). Camus sets great store by "dire" and "l'autre," because they form the basis for dialogue, that verbal buffer against divine dictation. Constructing limits around legitimate revolt is tantamount to self-preservation and the continuity of a social order. The rebel must not only oppose the oppressor but that part of himself which most resembles him. Fought on two fronts revolt replaces revolution which sees only the enemy outside. The result of seeing the oppressor as an alien force constitutes, in Camus' view, the fundamental basis of nihilism.

The term *nihilism* itself is used by Camus with its traditional meanings: the denial of objective grounds for human values and its necessary corollary, already examined in *Le Mythe de Sisyphe*, that life is meaningless; the belief that the human condition is or has become so intolerable as to make the destruction of all political and moral institutions worthwhile for its own sake, independent of any constructive social program; the specific, political program of a Russian party, including such figures as Pisarev and Bakounin, who advocated terrorism and assassination. To these several definitions Camus adds still another, the creation of a personal or political order dedicated, in the name of revolt and absolute freedom, to the systematic mutilation of human life, an organized anarchy whose contradictory terms are held together through the sheer will of one powerful personality. Camus isolates two nihilisms in Western history: "celui de l'individu et celui de l'Etat" (E, 539). The latter is characterized by totalitarianism, the concentration camp, and a strict adherence to the death penalty; the former stresses the abolition of one's personal past since the past represents human ties, obliging us to recognize that the self has been preceded, that it has consequently evolved and not been created. It also refers to the extreme individualism of the Marquis de Sade and his doctrine of justified murder, a doctrine adopted and developed by the romantics and surrealists, all of whom reiterate the self's non-negotiable demand for absolute freedom. The hyphen between personal and political nihilism is the conqueror or dictator. He owes nothing to the past of institutions or to his own. Camus can therefore write in an essay on Franco Spain published the same year as *L'Homme révolté*: "J'ai rencontré dans l'histoire . . . beaucoup de vainqueurs dont j'ai trouvé la face hideuse. Parce que j'y lisais la haine et la solitude. C'est qu'ils n'etaient rien quand ils n'étaient pas vainqueurs" (E, 1797).

Documenting the spread of totalitarian regimes in the nineteenth and twentieth century, Camus, in effect, is accusing the rebels of never having rebelled. In order to preserve the living evidence of revolt, and therefore its authenticity, the oppressor's status must be changed but his life preserved.[16] To the extent that the parent is an oppressor, the past too must be preserved. The result, depending on one's politics, is continuity or compromise. The doctrine of continuity, an adjustment that Camus brings to the doctrine of revolt, is summarized in his statement: "Je me révolte, donc nous sommes" (E, 432).

Historical analysis and personal introspection converge on this issue because Camus feels an urgent need to recognize his

16. Camus comments on the execution of Louis XVI: "Certes, c'est un répugnant scandale d'avoir présenté comme un grand moment de notre histoire l'assassinat public d'un homme faible et bon" (E, 528–29).

origins. That gaze turned back and within confronts him with his limitations to the extent that the past is always specific and concrete, never, like the future, fantastical, the product of "vouloir." Camus takes every opportunity to reaffirm, against others and against himself, his realistic humanity. A considerable portion of his vocabulary is deployed to enrich, through the use of synonyms, this central concept of origins: "racines," "personne," "mémoire," "psychologie," "garder," "collaborer," "réalité," "passé," "fidèle," "nature," "mère." Antonyms intensify this same theme through their opposition: "oublier," "personnage," "abstraction," "séquestré," "couper," "détruire," "rejeter," "avenir," "infidèle."[17] Camus also quotes Herzen, Kotliarevski, and Pisarev[18] who see the destruction of the past as a prerequisite for an emancipated future:

Herzen . . . faisant l'apologie du mouvement nihiliste . . . écrira: "L'annihilation du vieux, c'est l'engendrement de l'avenir." (E, 560)

Kotliarevski, parlant de ceux que l'on appelait aussi les radicaux, les définissait comme des apôtres, "qui pensaient qu'il fallait renoncer complètement au passé et forger sur un autre type la personnalité humaine." (E, 560)

Niant tout ce qui n'est pas la satisfaction de soi, Pisarev pose, sans rire, la question de savoir si l'on peut assommer sa mère, et répond: "Et pourquoi pas, si je le désire et si je le trouve utile?" (E, 561)

Judging from the massive evidence provided by Camus the suppression of the past, whether historical or psychological, engenders not an emancipated future but a bloody fiction, one where

17. Some examples include: "Le dandy se rassemble, se forge une unité. . . . Dissipé en tant que personne privée de règle, il sera cohérent en tant que personnage" (E, 462); "La révolte, coupée de ses vraies racines, infidèle à l'homme parce que soumise à l'Histoire, médite maintenant d'asservir l'univers entier" (E, 580); "La pensée révoltée ne peut . . . se passer de mémoire" (E, 431); "Celui qui rejette tout le passé, sans en rien garder . . . celui-là se condamne à ne trouver de justification que dans l'avenir" (E, 566); "Un moi dressé contre toutes les abstractions, devenu lui-même abstrait . . . à force d'être séquestré et coupé de ses racines" (E, 474).

18. Even in his middle age, Camus lamented his "puissante organisation pour l'oubli" (C, 2, 344).

a new political order or a new self is created not so much *ex nihilo*, where no one is harmed, but *ex omnibus*, out of human capital. Camus goes so far as to claim that every modern revolution has in fact contributed to the further enslavement of man.

Many artists figure in Camus' pantheon of rebels because the artist is the expert in creating fiction out of reality. That fiction, or imaginary reality, in turn corresponds to a third fundamental desire catalyzing revolt: "Dans toute révolte se découvre l'exigence métaphysique de l'unité, l'impossibilité de s'en saisir et la fabrication d'un univers de remplacement. . . . L'exigence de la révolte, à vrai dire, est en partie une exigence esthétique" (E, 659). The unity sought by the self, related to the "divine" appetite, is satisfied in art but only temporarily. A work of art exists within circumscribed limits where aesthetic problems, such as unity of composition, are proposed and resolved more or less successfully by each artist. Unlike reality which, in Camus' view, possesses neither a beginning nor an end, except in personal terms of one's birth and death, art embodies a closed universe where actions begin, end, and never change. Camus' critique of Christianity and Communism points out that what they view as art is reality itself. The Christian world boasts a Genesis and an Apocalypse, a divine comedy written by God. Hegelian/Marxist history posits a political goal, the ideal State, that is defined objectively and to which we must passively submit.[19] Objective Truth tolerates only consent. One does not believe in God or History, but, like Saint Paul's "Now ye are the body of Christ," one believes *in* God or *in* History. It is as if these deities, like Cronus and Uranus who devoured their children, could guarantee their personal future by eating it. We are not persons, partial agents in our own lives, but personages, passive agents of a transcendental author. Camus quotes the Catholic critic Stanislas Fumet who had stated that an author, in his creation, "fait une coupable concurrence à Dieu" (E, 662). Camus accepts the view of the artist seeking and exercising divine omniscience in his creation and that every work of art is a rebellion. Camus,

---

19. Camus considers Christianity more logical than Marxism: "Un mouvement auquel on refuse un commencement ne peut avoir de fin" (E, 628).

however, is not Catholic and the guilt, as we shall see, lies elsewhere.

What characterizes the evolution of aesthetics in the nineteenth and twentieth century, an evolution Camus attributes to the romantics and to the influence of Sade, is the gradual abolition of the line dividing formal fiction from formless reality. Camus himself had made it amply clear in *Le Mythe de Sisyphe* that whatever categories we may assign to human experience, or the moral and political restrictions we may place on the human personality in general and the artist in particular, are absolutely unjustified. He now attempts to modify that position. He recognizes that art is a distinct discipline imposing specific duties and offering the following rewards: "L'écrivain . . . n'a rien à se refuser. Pour lui, du moins, les limites s'écroulent et le désir peut aller jusqu'au bout" (E, 456). Further on Camus adds: "La dernière chose qu'un artiste puisse éprouver devant son art est le repentir" (E, 659). The key phrase is "devant son art" because reality, populated by persons and not personages, calls for compromise and, therefore, ethics. Camus' own novels are murderous but there is no guilt because there is no flesh. As early as 1942, Camus had written in his notebook: "Il faut imaginer une certaine distance de la création à l'acte. L'artiste veritable se trouve à mi-chemin de ses imaginations et de ses actes. C'est celui qui est 'capable de'" (C, 2, 20). Art, in this one respect, provides all the pleasures of vice and none of the responsibilities of virtue. Camus admits in the *Carnets*: "J'ai choisi la création pour échapper au crime" (C, 2, 253).

Exercising absolute authority within boundaries he himself has drawn, the artist, while alive, enjoys possession of his material that comes from the knowledge that his characters, devoid of energy, will, and choice, await their destiny. Also in 1942, Camus had stated: "Le créateur n'a rien à attendre d'une 'dictée' transcendante. *La Chartreuse, Phèdre, Adolphe* auraient pu être très différents—et non moins beaux. Cela dépendait de leur auteur—maître absolu" (C, 2, 37). In a work of art, therefore, movement and time cease; reality and doubt are conjugated into fiction, knowledge, and total possession. Describing art as a prison, Camus concludes: "Sur ces mondes fermés l'homme peut regner et connaître enfin" (E, 659).

The goal, however, of the post-Revolutionary artist is to extend his dominion beyond aesthetics, in Camus' words, to transform art "en expérience et en moyen d'action" (E, 490). The artist has become dangerous. He has abolished the distinction between his imaginary creation where he reigns supreme and the real world where he is, at best, a privileged citizen, a licensed sensibility. He seeks to exercise that control in reality which is his by right of professional authority in fiction. Poetry in action is a divine impulse that has abandoned aesthetic limits to overflow into the physical gestures of social intercourse. The artist, now lover, now politician, Don Juan or Caligula, synchronizes art and life.[20] Those individuals who enter his sphere of influence, like the citizens of God or History, Church, totalitarian state, or concentration camp, must surrender agency, ready to rhyme or risk being revised, perhaps erased like so many clumsy expressions.

The modern artist, now politically committed, seeks possession of persons and Camus points to Sade as the model of the writer/revolutionary who attempted to liberate the artist by thrusting him out of his conventional territory. Total possession signifies the investment of a person with the self's desire. Insofar as he or she can be said to be an ambassador of reality, thereby signifying change and death, the self, in suppressing the other person, authenticates its own immortality. At the same time, the self, seeking to transcend the human condition on a scale more ambitious than a work of art, finds it is dependent upon others when that supremacy, in order to be, must be demonstrated. The nihilistic solution is death or slavery because both, in different degrees, allow the artist *cum* politician or, like Don Juan, the artist *cum* lover, simultaneously to demonstrate its power and avoid the dependency that attends it. Thus destroyed or dehumanized, persons become little more than extensions of one self, in other words, fictional characters. Such a phenomenon, in Camus' view, goes beyond the violence that we at times inflict upon others, if by violence we mean something unpremeditated; it replaces the accidents of passion with an aes-

20. In 1952, Camus published his study of Oscar Wilde where he comments on the synthesis of art and life: "Wilde . . . avait tourné le dos à la réalité. . . . Son plus grand effort était de transformer sa vie même en oeuvre d'art et de vivre sous la seule loi de l'harmonie et du raffinement" (E, 1123).

thetic of atrocity, something systematic and permanent. The ultimate goal would be a master reigning over nonentities, a society without citizens, a frame encompassing a void whose title might be "And then there were none."

Camus feels it was perhaps inevitable that these ambitions, catalyzed by the French Revolution, were to prompt the artist, now discontent both with everyday life and with make-believe, not merely to revolt but to offer his allegiance to personal and social revolution, to become a nihilist. Art was no longer a *métier*, a commitment among other commitments and operating within laws that were spelled out clearly. Camus, for example, is able to equate the romantic doctrine of inspiration with nihilism because the former denied the resistance of rules against overwhelming passion while the latter denies the resistance of persons to one man's revolt. As if by a reverse military tactic, the nihilist scorches not the territory he abandons but the earth he conquers. Art was to be denied its privileged but limited status. Paradoxically, since the artist never ceased to think like an artist in other domains, art was allowed to dominate his life and the lives of others completely and without appeal to other experiences. Fiction was denounced but, as Camus knew, since he implicates himself, it was by such fictions as the perfect state, the perfect lover, the perfect man, absolute innocence or absolute guilt, or simply the notion, proposed in *Le Mythe*, that you can be whatever you wish to be, that the artist ignored or condemned reality altogether.

Committed nevertheless to himself as a writer, Camus attempts to formulate a new classicism, a doctrine which, through the reaffirmation of limits, would transform art from a paradigm of life into a privileged element in life. The artist "par nature"[21] opposed abstraction, not the abstraction that necessarily resides in art, the formal articulation of feelings and ideas prompted by experience, but the reverse process where experience itself acquires the formal attributes of art. For all intents and purposes, Camus considers Hegel and Marx as dangerous artists when, examining their theories of history, he demonstrates that for them: "La beauté sera vécue, non plus imaginée"

21. See p. 92.

(E, 658). If beauty is to be transferred to reality intact, then reality, always found wanting, will be destroyed. The legitimate artist, however, in Camus' words, collaborates with reality.[22] That reality includes not only the beauty in the world that the writer recognizes and leaves intact, be it alien to his taste, but society itself. Collaboration requires two things: a relationship with Nature based on contemplation and not manipulation; a contract between artist and public whose terms are subject to review with each publication. Camus is no more willing now to manipulate Nature than he is his mother's identity. The figure of the mother, particularly, is becoming fixed in a specific reality, such as the past, against which Camus can analyze and not invent his own nature. Discovering values in life seriously compromises how far you can go in manipulating life. As for the reader, the classical artist seeks to increase his capacity for feeling. As early as 1943, in his study of Mme de Lafayette entitled "L'Intelligence et l'échafaud," Camus commented on this point: "Il faut être deux quand on écrit. . . . Le grand problème est . . . la traduction de ce qu'on sent en ce qu'on veut faire sentir" (TRN, 1897). It is true that the writer's purpose is to bring the reader as close as possible to his own way of thinking. This self-serving enterprise is also considerably modified by the fact that the writer is two persons and that he has, during the gestation of his work, incorporated the reader's point of view, if only through the rules of language. The classical artist does not seek to impose his experiences but to negotiate them. His influence, moreover, is not direct, that is to say exercised on a person to person basis, but indirect, translated through the medium of the text. The classicist would accept Vautrin's statement in Le Père Goriot: "Je suis un grand poète. Mes poésies, je ne les écris pas: elles consistent en actions et en sentiments" as a rebellious impulse in human nature, not as a personal or social prescription. The text, instead, embodies a coded message which the reader is free to accept or reject, altogether or in part. Since art, in this respect, belongs to the public domain, the writer, through publication, severs his ties with his own vision, and the reader, through his private in-

---

22. "L'individu ne peut accepter l'histoire telle qu'elle va. Il doit détruire la réalité pour affirmer ce qu'il est, non collaborer avec elle" (E, 559–60).

terpretation (or misinterpretation), will claim it as his own. It is through publication that the writer who was "two" becomes again one, intimately separated from the reader who holds the book in his hand. One year before the publication of *L'Homme révolté*, in his essay "L'Enigme," Camus makes a powerful impression by stating the obvious: "Un écrivain écrit en grande partie pour être lu" (E, 862).

A work of art is in fact a microcosm corresponding to a desire for unity, for a suprahuman status, and it does transcend the formlessness of our lives. When it enters the reader's experience, however, it undergoes the necessary modifications to become a temporary, perishable, and therefore human pleasure, exercising its many powers and privileges within specific limits of time and space.

In an interview contemporary with *L'Homme révolté*, Camus summarizes an aesthetic that is classical but filtered through a romantic, nihilistic sensibility: "Connaissant bien l'anarchie de ma nature, j'ai besoin de me donner en art des barrières. Gide m'a appris à le faire. Sa conception du classicisme considéré comme un romantisme dompté est la mienne" (E, 1340). Romantic art blurred some of the distinctions and categories once taken for granted, such as the division of genres. In his last interview before his death, Camus, when asked what relationship there was between his works of fiction and nonfiction, replied: "J'écris sur des plans différents pour éviter justement le mélange des genres" (E, 1926). Camus wishes to restore that clarity which would derive not only from the classical notion of appropriate laws for separate genres but from the more personal notion of the separate and distinct categories of experience. The thrust of leftist thinking in France at this time was to merge the artist and the politician, to make one indistinguishable from the other. In a recent interview, Sartre summarizes a viewpoint that affects not only the artist and the politician but the even broader categories of the subjective and objective personality:

Selon moi, ce qui vicie les rapports entre les gens, c'est que chacun conserve par rapport à l'autre quelque chose de caché, de secret. . . . Je pense que la transparence doit se substituer en tout temps au secret, et j'imagine assez bien le jour où deux hommes n'auront plus de secrets l'un pour l'autre parce qu'ils n'en auront plus pour personne, parce que la vie subjective, aussi bien que la vie objective, sera totalement offerte, donnée.[23]

Camus, who shared these views *grosso modo* at the time he wrote *Le Mythe de Sisyphe*, wishes instead to distinguish the artist from the man in order to enhance their individual integrity, and he refuses to merge subjective and objective, the inner and public life. What Sartre calls "hidden" and "secret," Camus would call "private."

Sartre's romantic notion of transparency, which is synchronic, differs from Camus' classicism, which is analytical. Sartre, for example, refuses to believe that the adult is formed by the child: "Je ne crois pas que l'histoire d'un homme soit inscrite dans son enfance."[24] To do this would recognize limits on individual liberty and self-determination. Camus, on the other hand, insists on that past and that limitation.

The past barely exists in *Caligula* and *L'Etranger* and is denounced in *Le Mythe de Sisyphe*. With no past, innocence and freedom come easy. *L'Homme révolté*, however, makes every effort to restore the past in order to link each of us to a body of experience, such as our childhood, over which we had little or no control. In 1946, Camus wrote in his notebooks: "Un enfant n'est rien par lui-même. Ce sont ses parents qui le représentent" (C, 2, 177). Such a statement proves not our absolute freedom but our contingency, one that is not only lateral, such as our relationship with our contemporaries, but vertical, our once dependent relationship, in the past, with our parents. In terms of innocence and guilt, the results are closer to reality:

L'homme enfin n'est pas entièrement coupable, il n'a pas commencé l'histoire; ni tout à fait innocent puisqu'il la continue. Ceux qui passent cette limite et affirment son innocence totale finissent dans la rage de la culpabilité définitive. La révolte nous met au contraire sur le chemin d'une culpabilité calculée. (E, 700)

23. *Nouvel Observateur*, no. 554 (June 23–29, 1975), p. 72.
24. Ibid., no. 555 (June 30–July 6, 1975), p. 80.

In this respect, Sartre, in the same interview, illuminates another, perhaps the major difference between the two men: "Je ne me sens jamais coupable, et je ne le suis pas."[25] Classicism, therefore, resisting romantic and existentialist synthesis, constitutes more than an aesthetic. In alliance with revolt, it constitutes, for Camus, a moral option and an ethic.

It is Camus' ultimate purpose to affirm, against the thrust of the last two hundred years of Western history, against Sartre who claims that what we are is what we decide to be, against his own *Mythe de Sisyphe*, the existence of a human nature. He states his theme early in the book: "L'analyse de la révolte conduit au moins au soupçon qu'il y a une nature humaine, comme le pensaient les Grecs, et contrairement aux postulats de la pensée contemporaine" (E, 425). Camus is evidently opposing himself to Sartre's "situations" not because he does not believe in them, quite the contrary, but because he suspects that if all human experience is situational, that is to say public gestures, lucid and unfettered decisions, and an eternal present, then everything can be manipulated. If there are only situations, then the human personality rises to the body's surface to become, in Sartre's view, "transparent," in Camus', the creation of fantasy: "S'il n'y a pas de nature humaine, la plasticité de l'homme est, en effet, infinie" (E, 640).[26] But infinite malleability is too close to wishful thinking. Camus had already suspected as much in "L'Exil d'Hélène":

Depuis longtemps tout l'effort de nos philosophes n'a visé qu'à remplacer la notion de nature humaine par celle de situation. . . . Tandis que les Grecs donnaient à la volonté les bornes de la raison, nous avons mis . . . l'élan de la volonté au coeur de la raison, qui en est devenue meurtrière. (E, 855)[27]

Equating reason with limits, on the grounds that reason can never know everything, Camus puts will-power barely one step

25. Ibid., no. 556 (July 7–13, 1975), p. 72.
26. Further on Camus states again: "La révolution absolue supposait en effet l'absolue plasticité de la nature humaine" (E, 651).
27. In 1946, Camus had already written in his notes: "Tout l'effort de la pen-

removed from wish and illusion. The nihilist, the "willfull" man par excellence, is not, Camus reminds us, the man who believes in nothing, but the man who does not believe in "ce qui est" (E, 479). When "volonté" takes over "raison," the result is the belief in personal or political omnipotence. The paradoxical effect of all this is that those same thinkers, including Sartre, who deny childhood are, in Camus' view, fixated on childhood and its fantasies of power. Camus studies his past to become an adult. He told us in *Le Mythe* that he would join the Resistance and, choosing action over contemplation, become a man. That cue for action, however, was perhaps the not uncomfortable awareness that he did not know himself. Whereas, in *Le Mythe de Sisyphe*, he had mocked Socrates and the Socratic dialogue based on self-analysis and contradiction, he now affirms: "Platon a raison contre Moïse et Nietzsche. Le dialogue à hauteur d'homme coûte moins cher que l'évangile des religions totalitaires, monologué et dicté du haut d'une montagne solitaire" (E, 687). Camus realizes that his ignorance was calculated. We read in the penultimate sentence of *L'Homme révolté*: "A l'heure où naît enfin un homme il faut laisser l'époque et ses fureurs adolescentes" (E, 709).[28] To be a man is to be here and there, in the present and in the past, private and public, guilty and innocent, to be divided, limited, and therefore human. Camus will not accept the view that any specific situation, whether a political decision, a text, or conversation, could ever be, as Sartre would have it, consubstantial with one's total identity. *Le Mythe* proposed just such a heroic program only to be debunked in *La Peste*, in the person of Rieux. Camus himself, who had become the moral conscience of France, was expected to make his Orphic pronouncements on

---

sée allemande a été de substituer à la notion de nature humaine celle de situation humaine. . . . Comme les Grecs je crois à la nature" (C, 2, 174).

28. Camus more and more equates nihilism with adolescence: "Pisarev, théoricien du nihilisme russe, constate que les plus grands fanatiques sont les enfants et les jeunes gens" (E, 556); "Le conflit profond de ce siècle ne s'établit peut-être pas tant entre les idéologies allemandes de l'histoire et la politique chrétienne, qui d'une certaine manière sont complices, qu'entre les rêves allemands et la tradition méditerranéenne, les violences de l'éternelle adolescence et la force virile" (E, 702); "Notre civilisation se survit dans la complaisance d'âmes lâches ou haineuses, le voeu de gloriole de vieux adolescents" (E, 703–4).

every significant issue. Part of the impact of *L'Homme révolté* can be attributed to Camus' attempt to reclaim a private life, one that included the past which he was no longer willing to ignore or fictionalize.

If human nature exists, then the quest for freedom and self-determination requires coming to terms with other rebels. As a student of Hellenic thought Camus knew Aristotle's dictum that it takes two to have ethics. The solitary hero, like Patrice Mersault, Meursault, Caligula, Tarrou, in part Rieux, and soon Jean-Baptiste Clamence, becomes, therefore, an experiment to discover whether solitude is truly possible, or, as Daru will soon observe in "L'Hôte," not without displeasure, whether we have brothers, even if we do not love them. Solitude can be a flight from dangerous impulses, a lonely attempt to protect others; it is more often destructive, not the first but the last step in the gradual assimilation of all life into the ego. "Toute éthique de solitude," Camus writes, "suppose la puissance" (E, 447). Whereas the passage into manhood, to be authentic, depended upon the resistance of others, solitude, negating other lives, seeks divine transcendence.

Paraphrasing perhaps Sartre's famous line from *Huis-Clos*, "L'enfer c'est les autres," and as if to rehearse again the dispute between Rousseau and Diderot concerning self and society, the former convinced of his transparent innocence and self-sufficiency, the latter coming to terms with his flawed nature while examining his proper duties to society, Camus concludes: "Ce sont les autres qui nous engendrent. En société, seulement, nous recevons une valeur humaine, supérieure à la valeur animale" (E, 546). We are not surprised, therefore, that Camus calls revolt: "Mère des formes, source de vraie vie" (E, 704). He rediscovered his real mother. In contrast, the imperial self seeks to engender itself. Like a dramatic entrance on stage, it appears from nowhere. No matrix nourished it and, in turn, it nourishes nothing.

5 / Camus Anti-Camus: A Final Accounting

CAMUS gave his third novel a structure similar to his first. Divided into two parts, each leads to an act and explores the consequences of that act. The differences, however, are also striking. Whereas *L'Etranger* describes events in chronological order, *La Chute*, while advancing as a narrative, moves backward in time as its sole character, Jean-Baptiste Clamence, unfolds memory after memory until he reaches the episode that divides the book and his life, a woman's suicide on a bridge in Paris.

In a writer as self-aware as Camus these similarities and differences are not accidental. *La Chute* judges *L'Etranger*. It also judges Sartre, whose attacks inspired this book. Camus evaluates his mentor, his past, and himself; he offers the reader his final assessment of the imperial vision.

When Camus reviewed Sartre's *La Nausée* in 1938 he read it as a monologue rather than a novel and his distinction between these two forms offers much insight into Camus' evolution as an artist. *La Chute* exaggerates and satirizes the structure of

L'Etranger. By eschewing the first person narration in which all voices are subordinate to the voice of Meursault in favor of a monologue where Clamence alone speaks, Camus exposes the latent content of his first novel, the will to shape and reshape one's life until it transcends everyday reality.

Until the publication of *L'Homme révolté,* Camus had engaged in an intense debate with himself on the question of monologue and dialogue, and it ultimately focused on the participatory or dominating impulses of the self. What emerges is that Camus viewed these aesthetic forms as morally antithetical options. After the Occupation and a first-hand experience of Nazi dictatorship, the author of *Caligula* and *L'Etranger,* once infatuated with the power of unassailable truths and the soliloquies they embody, now laments: "Le long dialogue des hommes vient de s'arrêter" (E, 332). *La Peste* was an arduous attempt to fill gaps the author himself had helped to create. In political terms dialogue represented the democratic tradition of open intellectual exchange made vital by the tacit assumptions that no man possessed the truth entirely and that there was no entire truth to possess: "Le démocrate, après tout, est celui qui admet qu'un adversaire peut avoir raison, qui le laisse donc s'exprimer et qui accepte de réfléchir à ses arguments" (E, 320). Extremists, Camus complained, "ne croient pas à la persuasion" (C, 2, 159). As he later explains, persuasion, the ability to change someone's mind on a specific issue, has been replaced by intimidation, the practice of permanently neutralizing your opponent through fear and the threat of violence (E, 402). Clamence has his views but he does not practice persuasion because he believes that his views are absolutely correct and because there is no hard evidence that he is in fact speaking to anyone but himself. His monologue is the final step in the long process of liquidating one's opponent, so much so that Clamence feels free to expose his methods. He is not a fool. If he does so it is because he fears no reprisals:

Nous ne disons plus, comme aux temps naïfs: "Je pense ainsi. Quelles sont vos objections?" Nous sommes devenus lucides. Nous avons remplacé le dialogue par le communiqué. "Telle est la vérité, disons-nous.

Vous pouvez toujours la discuter, ça ne nous intéresse pas. Mais dans quelques années, il y aura la police qui vous montrera que j'ai raison." (TRN, 1498–99)

Camus implicates himself in this general condemnation. In the place of "Nos philosophes sont devenus" and "ils ont remplacé" he substituted the all-inclusive "nous sommes devenus" and "nous avons remplacé" (TRN, 2022).

If, on the other hand, Clamence is in fact speaking to some-one else, then the novel is all the more disturbing. The inter-locutor's presence is represented by invisible pauses in the text. Clamence first addresses him as "cher monsieur" and, passing through "mon cher compatriote," "cher ami," "cher," and "très cher," he proceeds to seduce him into total passivity. The lis-tener, finally addressed or mocked as "cher maître," is sup-pressed altogether when, in the novel's concluding paragraph, Clamence is able to say: "Prononcez vous-même les mots . . . que je dirai par votre bouche" (TRN, 1551). This person has become little more than a megaphone for a god-like voice.

Clamence is the fictional equivalent of the dictators Camus portrayed in *L'Homme révolté* and who, like them, could never survive the tensions of dialogue. Dialogue at least offers verbal sanity because wherever the speaker goes he will encounter in-terruptions, modifications, and limits. Camus' definition of the nihilist as one who does not believe in what exists constitutes an equally appropriate definition of a man who is insane. Caligula, Meursault, and Clamence, in varying degrees, are quite mad. They really do not hear because they cannot truly believe in the reality of the speaker, much less his words. They are propagan-dists and polemicists:

Il n'y a pas de vie sans dialogue. Et sur la plus grande partie du monde, le dialogue est remplacé aujourd'hui par la polémique. Le XXᵉ siècle est le siècle de la polémique et de l'insulte. . . . Des milliers de voix, jour et nuit, poursuivant chacune de son côté un tumultueux monologue, dé-versent sur les peuples un torrent de paroles. . . . Mais quel est le mécanisme de la polémique? Elle consiste à considérer l'adversaire en ennemi, à le simplifier par conséquent et à refuser de le voir. . . . Nous ne vivons plus parmi des hommes, mais dans un monde de silhouettes. (E, 401–2)

The process of abstraction, where the other person is denied any real presence on the level of intellectual discourse, the consequence of absolute convictions, can lead to liquidation. There is no guilt because nothing has been lost. Meursault's desire to disincarnate other people has become political. Camus had already engaged in several polemics when he wrote these lines in 1948, notably with François Mauriac and Emmanuel d'Astier de la Vigerie, and he gave as much as he got. The dispute with Sartre, however, was something quite different. Now Camus was opposed to a man with whom he had been intimate. It is as if, for the first time, Camus winced at the wounds he inflicted. *La Chute*, therefore, would go one step further than the historically oriented *L'Homme révolté* and become a much more personal exposé of himself and Sartre.

The oversimplification that dehumanizes other people reflects, in the final analysis, the oversimplified opinion the speaker has of himself. There is no life, Camus said, without dialogue, another way of saying that life is unthinkable without conflict. Monologue creates a climate of abstraction because it proceeds from one. Caligula "knows"; Tarrou "knows"; Meursault is serene compared to everyone else[1] and he "never lies"; *Le Mythe de Sisyphe* imagines conflicts only between "I" and "the world." It is really with *La Peste*, with Bernard Rieux, that doubts set in and characters are willing to listen because they are in conflict with themselves. Like their author they again have something to learn. Dialogue first requires inner dialogue, and it is through such breaches in the human psyche that other people can enter: "Chaque adversaire, si répugnant soit-il, est une de nos voix intérieures que nous serions tentés de faire taire" (E, 1716). The suppression of others amounts to a suppression of a part of oneself, the human part where conflict is inevitable. There is really no conflict in Clamence. "L'essentiel est que tout devienne

---

1. One article sees Meursault as an Oriental sage: Leonard N. Sugden, "Meursault, an Oriental Sage," *French Review* 6 (1974), 196–207.

simple, comme pour l'enfant" (TRN, 1545), he declares after he had already concluded: "Il a fallu . . . découvrir enfin que je n'étais pas simple" (TRN, 1518). Clamence is not Camus precisely because he reverses the order of Camus' discoveries about his own self. The monologue in *La Chute* is certainly Camus' confession but that confession includes the satirical distance that Camus can put between himself and his character, between himself and his past.

That crucial distance also permits Camus to judge Sartre. He does so by giving Clamence intellectual views Sartre expressed in his works and then exposing their moral and political consequences: the master-slave relationship which Sartre accepted as the essential human relationship in *L'Etre et le néant* and which Clamence uses to justify the totalitarian state; the attack on memory in *Huis-Clos* and *Les Mouches* through which a man can proclaim his freedom from moral judgments. Camus also uses the form and content of *La Nausée* directly and critically in *La Chute*.

Roquentin's boast, "Je ne reçois rien, je ne donne rien"[2] applies to Clamence. *La Nausée* and *La Chute* dramatize the lives of two men who willfully and systematically abandon their human ties, including their profession, their middle-class origins, books, loves, to name only a few. They abandon language itself. It is barely tolerable to Roquentin, who finds that words mask reality and who, by a kind of preciosity in reverse, finds only obscenity liberating; language is tolerable to Clamence on the condition that no one else speaks. Divine simplicity, to be uniquely one, is their goal. They must cut themselves off from all associations and, what is far more difficult, from the memory of all associations. To be inhabited even by the images of other people would muddy an otherwise flawless self.

What is absent in *La Nausée*, however, is mockery. Judging from recent interviews, Sartre, until his death, believed in Roquentin the way Camus once believed in Meursault. He believed, for example, that Roquentin is truly an innocent bystander as he watches a homosexual being trapped into seducing a boy. "Que

2. Jean-Paul Sartre, *La Nausée* (Paris: Gallimard, 1970), p. 17.

pouvais-je faire?"[3] he asks. Himself the object once of the man's advances, Roquentin's hatred and fears at that time were so overwhelming that he was tempted to plunge a knife into the man's eye. When the homosexual becomes someone else's victim, however, it is sympathy and outrage that flow from his pen, never complicity.

Camus, who dealt with the notion of the innocent bystander much more sympathetically in *L'Etranger*, abandons it altogether in *La Chute*. Instead, he has arranged for the victim to act out Clamence's misogynist fantasy. An expression employed by the homosexual in *La Nausée* very likely influenced Camus' decision to have the girl commit suicide by throwing herself into the Seine. In this manner, his novel would be a direct comment on Sartre's:

> L'autodidacte se rapprocha jusqu'à me souffler au visage:
> "Si vous vouliez, monsieur? . . ."
> "Quoi donc?"
> Il rougit et ses hanches ondoyèrent gracieusement:
> "Monsieur, ah! monsieur: je me jette à l'eau. Me feriez-vous l'honneur de déjeuner avec moi mercredi?"[4]

A banal expression from *La Nausée* is transformed into a dramatic crisis in *La Chute*. Whereas the girl's death by drowning takes place halfway through the novel, the homosexual's public disgrace occurs near the end of Roquentin's journal, at about the time he decides to leave Bouville for Paris. Camus wants us to see the consequence of Clamence's unwillingness to try to save the woman and to demonstrate that his innocence was a self-serving illusion. Sartre reinforces Roquentin's innocence throughout the entire sordid affair. Society has no use for the homosexual and Roquentin has no use for either of them. As Roquentin leaves, he concludes his journal with the line: "Demain il pleuvra sur Bouville."[5] *La Chute* describes Clamence's de-

---

3. Ibid., p. 231.
4. Ibid., p. 110.
5. Ibid., p. 251.

cision to leave Paris for rainsoaked Amsterdam. It begins where *La Nausée* left off. The contrast, however, is ironical because Camus is telling Roquentin and Sartre that they never left Bouville.

The distance between Camus and Sartre provides one more bit of evidence of the distance between Camus and his past. Not that he is disavowing his origins, merely the youth who claimed the past did not exist. From the postwar years until his death we see Camus gradually and with increasing fervor reaffirming his debt to those who formed him. In the last years he wrote essays on figures who were important in his personal and intellectual life, as if to focus on the roots that nourished him. We already knew about Nietzsche and Dostoevsky but now there is "Rencontre avec Gide" (1951); "Herman Melville" (1952); "L'Artiste en prison" (an essay on Oscar Wilde published in 1952); "Roger Martin du Gard" (1955); "René Char" (1958); "Sur *Les Iles* de Jean Grenier" (1959). Between 1953 and 1959 Camus adapts plays of Pierre de Larivey, Pedro Calderón de la Barca, Dino Buzzati, Lope de Vega, Faulkner's *Requiem for a Nun* and Dostoevsky's *The Possessed*. In 1958 he agrees to reedit the biographical essays in *L'Envers et l'endroit*: "Pour moi, je sais que ma source est dans *L'Envers et l'endroit*, dans ce monde de pauvreté et de lumière où j'ai longtemps vécu" (E, 6). That world lives again in some of the stories from *L'Exil et le royaume* published in 1957, notably *Les Muets* and parts of *La Femme adultère* and *L'Hôte*. The confluence of these two works, one past, one present, balances Clamence's inhuman aria. Camus also undertook at the same time to write what he considered to be his first novel, the autobiographical *Le Premier homme*.

The tragedy during those years was France's eventual disavowal, during the Algerian crisis, of the country Camus considered inseparable from his identity. A citizen of both France and Algeria, Camus tried to mediate between opponents who wanted to forget the other existed. His panic is evident in his portrait of Clamence, a man without a country. If Camus chose to live in Paris, however, Clamence chooses to live in Limbo. Clamence rejects all national ties to become his own kingdom. *La Chute* was originally intended to form part of *L'Exil et le royaume*. Although published separately because of its length, the connection remains because Camus now sees exile, or emptiness, as the precondition of divinity. *La Chute* also stands out from the other stories because it demonstrates that the disassociation from human ties remains ineffective unless the mechanism by which they are formed, memory itself, is suppressed.

Memory is the faculty Clamence opposes with all the power of his considerable intelligence. Meursault killed but, living from day to day, he quickly became a stranger to the deed and to society's condemnation. Clamence only witnesses the suicide and is not legally responsible for the woman's death. He, however, lives to acquire, much against his will, a nagging memory of his inaction and to experience, much to his surprise, the discomforts of guilt. That memory would strike the reader as the height of improbability had Clamence not already admitted that he was two men, one of whom had the capacity to forget, to live, like Meursault, for the moment, and to enjoy his unfettered nature. He refers to this division in his nature when he describes his talents as a lawyer and particularly his benevolent feelings towards widows and orphans. They are his principal clients because, in terms of society's clichés, they are synonyms of innocence: "Je jouissais . . . de cette partie de ma nature qui réagissait si exactement à la veuve et à l'orphelin qu'elle finissait, à force de s'exercer, par régner sur toute ma vie" (TRN, 1486). It is not clear at first what the other part could be until after the suicide, until Clamence hears derisive laughter at his back and somewhere inside of himself and slowly rediscovers that he is also endowed with a memory and a bad conscience.

"Le coeur a sa mémoire" (TRN, 1478) Clamence states in the novel's opening pages, and by this Pascalian admission, he places memory, for the time being, beyond the reach of wishful thinking. When he adds: "Le désir . . . où je suis de bien vous faire comprendre cette ville, et le coeur des choses! Car nous sommes au coeur des choses" (TRN, 1482–83), he informs us that his monologue will coincide with his many walks through the "concentric" and "infernal" canals of Amsterdam and that his self-analysis will accuse and reflect a dying civilization.

Clamence offers this maxim: "Quand on n'a pas de caractère

il faut bien se donner une méthode" (TRN, 1481).[6] Method refers to an abstract life, that is to say a life organized, controlled, and directed by one clearly defined purpose. A method, therefore, can be "given to oneself" or imposed on someone else. Nothing must be left to experience since experience includes chance. "Caractère" is the antithesis of method because it embodies a complete psychological constellation including instincts and desires that can be dealt with but not denied, as well as a memory that allows experiences to accumulate and the past to exist. As a result, what the individual gives to himself comes out of what was first given. "Caractère" is anything but immaculate because it raises memory to an inner principle of reality.

Although Clamence appears to be an outsider, an alien, it is appearance only because he argues for what society is becoming. His particular tragedy and our collective one is not only his refusal ever to acquire the dimensions of character but his decision to suppress the character born in him after the woman's suicide.

When Clamence talks about himself and his life in Paris, he evokes a personage, not a person. The personage is the physical embodiment of method. It is to character what fiction is to reality, and it is fiction by reason of its entire self-definition. Clamence's description of Paris, "un vrai trompe-l'oeil, un superbe décor habité par quatre millions de silhouettes" (TRN, 1478), literally sets the stage for a life that, like a rehearsed script, should hold no surprises. Clamence's self-possession is absolute and his divinity is in his method of which the book is a demonstration. Clamence's social satire is ferocious and always on target: "Silhouettes" is an apt term for anonymous residents of a city. These shadows, however, are also very much in the eye of this beholder.[7] Whoever comes into contact with Clamence suffers disincarnation and he admits that this draining process is made possible essentially by his ability to forget:

6. Camus has struck here a variation of this phrase in his introduction to *L'Homme révolté*: "A partir du moment où, faute de caractère, on court se donner une doctrine, dès l'instant où le crime se raisonne, il prolifère comme la raison elle-même, il prend toutes les figures du syllogisme" (E, 413).

7. "Silhouettes" had already appeared in Camus' speech, "Le Témoin de la li-

J'avais toujours été aidé par un étonnant pouvoir d'oubli. J'oubliais tout. . . . Ça glissait. Oui, tout glissait sur moi. (TRN, 1500–1)

Les êtres suivaient, ils voulaient s'accrocher, mais il n'y avait rien, et c'était le malheur. Pour eux. Car, pour moi, j'oubliais. (TRN, 1501)

"Il n'y avait rien," like Roquentin's "je ne reçois rien," describes a life constructed around a void where memories and recognition scenes would normally operate. Meursault's frequent use of indirect responses to direct questions has been carried to its extreme form, a man's capacity for indifference that, taking the form of an uninterrupted monologue, not only avoids people and their demands but excludes them altogether. There are no more questions. Clamence is Meursault grown to middle-age.

That void, however, is also a barrier serving to protect Clamence. To live his life, and only his life, he must have a memory of himself that would carry him from day to day. He admits: "Je ne me suis jamais souvenu que de moi-même" (TRN, 1501); "Moi, moi, moi, voilà le refrain de ma chère vie" (TRN, 1500). This memory is required to assist Clamence in his self-absorption. If he is to admire his reflection, something must appear, first to be recognized and then to be loved. It is moreover essential that Clamence not view his life as an organic process of growth because such a view would indicate that at some point in time he was incomplete. There can be no rites of passage for a god. Consequently, Clamence twice affirms his miraculous birth: "Je n'ai jamais eu besoin d'apprendre à vivre. Sur ce point, je savais déjà tout en naissant" (TRN, 1489); "Certains matins, je l'avoue humblement, je me sentais fils de roi, ou buisson ardent" (TRN, 1490). However much we may feel that there is madness in this method, method is all there is. Camus offers us a paradoxical situation where the function of memory is to support and preserve a perfect nature and in that capacity to forget completely whatever persons or situations that might contaminate that image. Only in this way can reality reside entirely within one supreme self. The only possible change for a god is to become human and therefore imperfect.

---

berté": "Devenus aux trois quarts aveugles par la grâce de la polémique, nous ne vivons plus parmi les hommes, mais dans un monde de silhouettes" (E, 402).

Such a change does take place. The suicide catalyzes a different kind of self-awareness in Clamence, one that is critical and cumulative and the novel records what could conceivably be called a psychoanalytical autobiography. Clamence may also be lying. He admits that he has not given his real name. *La Chute*, however, is a post-Freudian novel and we hear a liar telling the truth in the elaboration of his lies. A change did take place in Clamence which threatened to topple him from his Olympian heights. But rather than accept his active passivity, his complicity in the girl's suicide, rather than remain in the middle ground of humanity with its ration of vices and virtues, Clamence pushes his "fall" further still and becomes another god. In this sense the book's title is ironic; Clamence's "fall," like the woman's, was a leap. Enthroned like Satan in the lowest point in Europe, he holds court in a bar named Mexico City, the highest city in the world.[8] When the novel ends Clamence has not really changed. Once a deity inhabiting heights, he decides that he prefers, unlike Achilles, to be a king in hell rather than a man on earth.

Clamence attributes his fall directly to the woman's suicide. It is after that incident that he begins to acquire a memory that is not purely self-serving. Now when he contemplates himself it is no longer perfection that he sees. His inaction forces upon him the knowledge that as a god he was in fact dependent upon that same society over which he reigned, that what he considered, in his own words, a social machine designed for divine intervention was a reality designed to destroy gods:

Je vivais impunément. Je n'étais concerné par aucun jugement, je ne me trouvais pas sur la scène du tribunal, mais quelque part, dans les cintres, comme ces dieux que, de temps en temps, on descend, au moyen d'une machine, pour transfigurer l'action et lui donner son sens. (TRN, 1488)

Camus explores in this passage whether it is the god who initiates the action or the machine that is bringing him down. Sim-

---

8. According to *L'Homme révolté*, Clamence would qualify as an atheistic mystic: "C'est la recherche du sommet-abîme, familier aux mystiques. En vérité, il s'agit d'un mysticisme sans Dieu" (E, 506).

ilarly, Clamence, who tells us that he often fantasizes about killing people, was outdistanced by the woman who jumped off the
bridge. Sole witness, Clamence became helpless because the cue
for action was in other people, in his public. The actor becomes
a most ordinary man when the audience goes home. If he is
nothing but an actor, or a god, then no one remains. In a sense,
the woman was always alone. After telling his listener about a
mother forced by a Nazi to decide which of her two sons would
be killed as a hostage, Clamence adds: "Toutes les surprises sont
possibles" (TRN, 1481). The suicide was just such a surprise and
surprises underscore a lack of foresight. They reaffirm Clamence's distrust of experience. He reacquires that foresight
and, with an expressive use of the word *but*, he concludes: "Je
règne enfin, mais pour toujours" (TRN, 1548).

When he passes the woman on the bridge late at night, he responds to her presence and becomes sexually aroused by a brief
glimpse of her neck. Having just left his mistress he decides to
walk on. The woman's leap, therefore, is not only an unexpected event but a satire of his omnipotence, a blow to his mas-
culine pride. Her death mocks his desires because she is the one
who got away. Clamence then relates through association other
surprises that he thought were extinct in his mind: a mistress's
remark to mutual friends about his impotency; his dispute with
a cyclist in which, caught off guard, he is struck and publicly hu-
miliated. In each instance Clamence failed to live up to his own
notion of omnipotence. Responding with retrospective rage, he
is forced to recognize his violent feelings concerning humanity
in general and women in particular, a violence in direct ratio to
his unrealistic assumptions about himself and the world. It is
not only Clamence's ability to forget that is at issue here but also
his belief that memory could be trained, through sheer will, to
bend itself to one object of contemplation, Clamence himself.
He is totalitarian, all method and no content. In this respect,
Meursault and Tarrou are his immediate ancestors.

We can say that Clamence acquires a memory because he is
able to describe his past to us, however fictionalized that past
may be. What he actually discovers after the woman's death is
that all those incidents detrimental to his profoundest self-

image were suppressed, not forgotten. The simplicity he had enjoyed as a benevolent deity has been replaced by the contradictions of a flawed man:

> Je ne me reconnaissais que des supériorités, ce qui expliquait ma bienveillance et ma sérénité. Quand je m'occupais d'autrui, c'était pure condescendance, en toute liberté. . . . Avec quelques autres vérités, j'ai découvert ces évidences peu à peu, dans la période qui suivait le soir dont je vous ai parlé. Pas tout de suite, non, ni très distinctement. Il a fallu d'abord que je retrouve la mémoire. Par degrés, j'ai vu plus clair, j'ai appris un peu de ce que je savais. (TRN, 1500)

> Peu à peu la mémoire m'est cependant revenue. Ou plutôt je suis revenu à elle, et j'y ai trouvé le souvenir qui m'attendait. (TRN, 1501)

A brief encounter with a stranger becomes, for Clamence, an encounter with himself. When he tells us that he learned what he already knew, he is not indulging in self-glorification. On the contrary, Clamence is this time giving his full attention to certain facts about his nature. To pay attention, however, is not necessarily to accept. Memories of events and of his actions during those events eventually gather themselves into a pattern and replace an abstract and flawless method with a concrete personality. Clamence finds that human nature whose existence Camus suspected in *L'Homme révolté*. At no time does Camus claim that there is a one and universal human nature. He is increasingly convinced, however, of what Sartre categorically denied, that the process of psychological formation, while taking place in the present, begins to accumulate in each individual up until such time when, out of this material and within its limits, he can begin to form himself. Camus' sense of a nature that is human is essentially based on the existence in each one of us of an ineradicable past. All of Clamence's conclusions concerning his now debunked divinity explore this crucial link between memory and self-knowledge:

> Après de longues études sur moi-même, j'ai mis au jour la duplicité profonde de la créature. J'ai compris alors, à force de fouiller dans ma

mémoire, que la modestie m'aidait à briller, l'humilité à vaincre et la vertu à opprimer. Je faisais la guerre par des moyens pacifiques et j'obtenais enfin, par les moyens du désintéressement, tout ce que je convoitais. (TRN, 1518)

The crisis that emerges from this revelation is the choice Clamence must now make concerning the future direction of life. Having discovered his personality, he finds himself merely a part of that reality which he had always assumed existed entirely within himself.

The web of personal and social obligations, however, spun out of human strengths and weaknesses and which enmesh all members of society, is intolerable to him. Clamence, therefore, makes a crucial decision. He decides that he was never a mere man playing god but a god who was ignorant of his true nature. What could have been the cue for comedy, as in Marivaux's "Je vois clair dans mon coeur," ends up as tragedy. Clamence thought he was a benevolent providence succoring widows and orphans; he was instead, he decides, a malevolent deity. In his second and last incarnation, he is Satan. He takes on this new identity and the book dramatizes this reversal. He is simple again. The reversal is so complete, however, that it cancels itself out. Still a god, Clamence can claim: "Je n'ai pas changé de vie, je continue de m'aimer et de me servir des autres" (TRN, 1548).

La Chute is Camus' confession but it is at this point that he and Clamence diverge. If an author's works testify at all to his inner life, then Camus changed. He wrote in "Retour à Tipasa": "Retrouver cette force, jusqu'à présent fidèle, qui m'aide à accepter ce qui est, quand une fois j'ai reconnu que je ne pouvais le changer" (E, 870). This voyage, both real and symbolic, that Camus took to his home and into his past confirmed the nature of his character, part of which belonged to him, another part to his predecessors. It now becomes a question of equilibrium and Camus wrote his last books, in his own words, under the sign of Nemesis, goddess of moderation. Fidelity to the past becomes a paradigm of one's place in the present and in society. Accepting the Nobel prize, Camus offered his audience this complex appraisal of the self and its identity:

La réalité d'une vie d'homme ne se trouve pas seulement là où il se tient. Elle se trouve dans d'autres vies qui donnent une forme à la sienne, vies d'êtres aimés, d'abord . . . mais vies aussi d'hommes inconnus, puissants, et misérables . . . humbles représentants, enfin, du hasard souverain qui règne sur les existences les plus ordonnées. (E, 1086)

Clamence does not accept what he is; rather he glorifies in what he interprets as a sign of strength, the triumph of his method over his character, of total control over chance and experience. He demonstrates his ability to give the appearance of moving ahead when in fact, like the canals of Amsterdam and the circles of hell, he merely moves ahead to the same point.

Although memory may serve ethics and justice, Clamence is a lawyer who places himself above the law. A professional who is alien to the subject matter of his profession, he practices a doctrine of *lex gratia legis*, of flawless form over troubling content. Since one of the preoccupations of law is the relative presence of guilt and innocence in a person or situation, Clamence, like the heroes of *Le Mythe de Sisyphe* who "represent" the people, makes himself invulnerable to law in the arena of judgment. He does so by accepting innocence and guilt only as absolute terms and by applying them exclusively to himself. He becomes, as a result, the repository of justice, the ideal of which all else is an imperfect reflection, and he achieves through active self-interest what Meursault sought through indifference. A member of the establishment, Clamence is able, through professional expertise, to transform his status of citizen into that of ruler and to pursue in society the autonomy Meursault could only enjoy in prison. He puts the matter bluntly: "L'essentiel est de pouvoir tout se permettre" (TRN, 1548).

Clamence is a childless bachelor and widows and orphans are his preferred clients. A stranger to their lives and their loss, he directs his energies to those members furthest removed from his sphere. The further removed the client, the more rhetorical or abstract his participation, the more words take the place of deeds and personal risks. Clamence is all words and the quantum of energy he actually dispenses is therefore minimal: "J'avançais ainsi à la surface de la vie, dans les mots en quelque sorte, jamais dans la réalité" (TRN, 1501). This passage resembles Camus' evaluation of his youth in North Africa which he wrote shortly before his death: "Nous vivions ainsi dans la sensation, à la surface du monde, parmi les couleurs, les vagues, la bonne odeur des terres" (E, 1157). Abstraction is the common denominator of these two descriptions. Camus suggests that the division of sensation and intellect spawns cultural barbarism or sterility. Words too, like colors and odors, can become pure structures when they are permanently divorced from the rest of human experience. We may enter these structures provided we first divest ourselves of our unresolved humanity.[9]

The rhetoric Clamence displays in the courts gives only the appearance of human proximity with the individuals involved. He keeps a chaste distance and his gestures mimic reality.

The absurdist ideal of "absolute feigning" is reincarnated in Clamence, except this time in the context of an author who condemns it. Camus has Clamence choose widows and orphans because they have in common dead fathers and husbands. Working against Clamence, Camus places at the heart of the book those issues of relative innocence and guilt that its only character considers irrelevant to his life. Clamence's status as confirmed bachelor and Don Juan makes him an accomplice in the creation of husbandless wives and fatherless children because he views his pleasures abstractly, free from procreation and its network of responsibilities. At the same time, Camus makes the reader sense that something in Clamence responds to these women and children, that his "fatherliness" is more than a role, and that his "feigning" taps a very real longing. We get brief glimpses of the character Clamence wishes to suppress.

The question arises whether Clamence ever knows himself. The answer is ultimately negative because self-knowledge too contaminates the self's purity. After *Le Mythe de Sisyphe*, it took Camus several years to reevaluate Socrates' "know thyself" as

9. Camus rejected an interviewer's notion that *La Chute* was directly related to the stylistic innovations of such "new" novelists as Sarraute and Robbe-Grillet. The abstract qualities of *La Chute* were appropriate to the character, not the author (E, 1927).

the only valid prerequisite, however flawed, for realistic assessments of oneself and for any kind of change. Through an aroused memory Clamence gains considerable insight into himself, but before it is too late, before he must accept what he is, he leaves for Amsterdam and becomes Jean-Baptiste Clamence. Clamence knows Clamence, but Clamence is a fiction. He tells his listener: "Pour que la statue soit nue, les beaux discours doivent s'envoler" (TRN, 1511). He is supposed to be confessing· but where we expect "homme" we read "statue." Confession does not become an unsparing examination of what is but rather a calculated fantasy of what should be.

Camus claimed that *La Peste* was a confession and that he would tell everything he knew in *L'Homme révolté*. Clamence, however, makes this accusation: "Les auteurs de confessions écrivent surtout pour ne pas se confesser, pour ne rien dire de ce qu'ils savent" (TRN, 1538). It is extremely probable that these are Camus' sentiments as well but not for the same reasons. Clamence feels that authors of confessions lie. When Camus, on the other hand, looked back over his novels in 1950, he made this shrewd observation: "Des êtres sans mensonges, donc non réels. Ils ne sont pas au monde. C'est pourquoi . . . je ne suis pas un romancier au sens où on l'entend" (C, 2, 325). If these characters are without lies it is because they view themselves that way, all of a piece and always telling the truth. They are not of this world because of their extraordinary self-possession and because of the sure grip the author himself has on them. He, too, in his own way, did not want to be part of this world. To tell the truth always is an inhuman achievement. As late as 1955 Camus points to Meursault because he refuses to lie, calling him for this reason "le seul Christ que nous méritions" (TRN, 1929).

La Chute is a satire of "persons without lies" and of Meursault because Clamence is all lies. Unlike a man who lives his life, Clamence interprets his and that so completely that he leaves little for us to do. Play is impossible, having been replaced by play-acting. Consummate artist, Clamence uses the truth about himself not as an end but as a means to an end, to distort himself beyond recognition and to become inaccessible, a disembodied voice. It hardly matters, therefore, that Clamence changes from God to Satan, since the absolute innocence of one and the absolute guilt of the other have little to do with the human condition. In this respect, Clamence's references to Christ are quite revealing. Christ, the God become man, is an embarrassment to men moving in the opposite direction. "Devenir Dieu" was one of the rallying cries in *Le Mythe de Sisyphe*. Christ, however, represented too many ambiguities. Making his own bid for divinity, Jean-Baptiste Clamence undertakes to destroy the very person he, John the Baptist, is supposed to announce. Camus, on the other hand, who once defined Christ as a man who had become God, now sees him as a false god who became a man. That manhood which, in *Le Mythe de Sisyphe*, was merely a point of departure is now the goal. Clamence too proclaims Christ's humanity but for a different purpose. He destroys Christ's divinity in order to reaffirm his own. He can think of no better way to perform this task than to provide Christ with a memory:

> Savez-vous pourquoi on l'a crucifié? . . . A côté des raisons qu'on nous a très bien expliquées pendant deux mille ans, il y en avait une grande à cette affreuse agonie. . . . La vraie raison est qu'il savait, lui, qu'il n'était pas tout à fait innocent. S'il ne portait pas le poids de la faute dont on l'accusait, il en avait commis d'autres, quand même il ignorait lesquelles. Les ignorait-il d'ailleurs? Il était à la source, après tout; il avait dû entendre parler d'un certain massacre des innocents. Les enfants de la Judée massacrés pendant que ses parents l'emmenaient en lieu sûr, pourquoi étaient-ils morts sinon à cause de lui? Il ne l'avait pas voulu, bien sûr. Ces soldats sanglants, ces enfants coupés en deux, lui faisaient horreur. Mais, tel qu'il était, je suis sûr qu'il ne pouvait les oublier. (TRN, 1532–33)

Clamence has calculated his effects here very carefully. Children die when a god is born because divinity denies that entire range of formative experience. Exterminating angels or soldiers are the agents of gods and kings. If Christ were only a man, he could view the massacre as a monstrous tragedy and his good conscience would remain intact. As a man who thinks he is a god, however, he is directly responsible for a murder he himself set in motion but did not personally commit. As a god who became a man, he has acquired a memory, which makes absolute innocence, or guilt, impossible. The ability to forget is what sep-

arates gods from men. The question that confronts Clamence is
what to do with the memory that a woman's suicide aroused,
with the burden of a specific guilt which, unlike Christ, the god-
man, he has no intention of carrying.

The second half of *La Chute* describes Clamence's efforts to
put the woman's suicide out of his mind. His efforts include sexual orgies, which he hopes will dull his sensations, his ability to
feel and to respond to the pain of conscience. Like Don Juan, he
is both promiscuous and ascetic because the goal is to control the
body, if not abolish it altogether. Responding to the world, the
body allows the world to enter the mind. The ultimate achievement would be to exclude from the self anything that is not the
self. Taking his place in a tradition that goes back at least to
Rousseau's *Rêveries du promeneur solitaire*, Clamence is convinced
that the self grows by what it excludes, that the self is inexhaust-
ible and, like the snake with its proverbial tail in its mouth, can
feed on itself for eternity.

The memory of the suicide and of his inaction persists, however, and Clamence concludes bitterly that he is not yet "cured"
of the human condition. His tactic then is to use the memories
he cannot obliterate. It is at this crucial point that Clamence becomes both a judge-penitent[10] and an author: "Je m'accuse, en
long et en large. Ce n'est pas difficile, j'ai maintenant de la
mémoire" (TRN, 1547). This self-accusation is not the same
thing as self-analysis, which is an ongoing process, although elements of the latter must be brought in to provide verisimilitude.
The judge-penitent and author have stopped time. The number
of memories is reduced to a select few and there will be no more.
Part of the truth is conveyed to hide the entire truth, and guilt
merely serves to bring into focus the apparent authenticity of a
man apparently confessing. Clamence's avowed goal as a judge-
penitent is to inspire his listener to make his own confession. He
gains thereby the superiority he is always seeking: "Plus je

10. The idea of joining opposites, as in "juge-pénitent" was probably suggested to Camus by Sartre's attack in "Réponse à Albert Camus." Camus stated in
L'Homme révolté that he spoke "au nom de cette misère qui suscite des milliers
d'avocats et jamais un seul frère." Sartre then asked: "Vous qui parlez en son
nom, êtes-vous son avocat, son frère, son frère avocat?" *Situations*, 4 (Paris: Gallimard, 1964), 93.

m'accuse et plus j'ai le droit de vous juger" (TRN, 1548). His superiority resides in the fact that our confession may well be sincere while his is surely false.

Clamence, moreover, has set his speech down in writing and his identity, like a performance, is now fixed. He will never be caught off guard again and there will be no more surprises. Clamence is the author of a play in which he is the only character. Telling it all fills only so many pages and Clamence, unlike Camus, is a one book author. He is pure make-believe, the art of living now only art. Having aborted the human and ethical character that a woman's death helped create, he is relieved and royally calm.

In his final assessment of Clamence, Camus offers in evidence the fact that the woman's death reenacted Clamence's wish. She was there; he was aroused; and she died.

Women, generally, are the major victims in Camus' works. A sister dies in *Caligula*; then a mother in *L'Etranger*; a wife is exiled in *La Peste*; and a woman drowns herself in *La Chute*. Not only are women victims, they have, up till now, been virtually excluded as characters except when they assumed a male-oriented symbolic role as mother or lover. *La Chute* dramatizes this victimization and this exclusion more forcefully than any of the previous works because Camus is willing now to gain full access to the deepest implications of the imperial vision, to make manifest through Clamence the latent assumption in all his major works that empires require the death of women.

Don Juan, for whom women existed superficially, to satisfy his physical needs, embodied the promiscuous, political, activist life Camus idealized in *Le Mythe de Sisyphe* and *Combat*. Many of Clamence's pronouncements on love do in fact paraphrase statements made by Camus in *Le Mythe de Sisyphe* and in his private notebooks. He too, for example, enumerates and imagines countless female conquests. However, it would be incorrect, in my view, to assume that Clamence is only another disciple of Don Juan. His paraphrasing of the Don Juan method of seduction serves merely as a point of departure. If Clamence is an "explanation" of Don Juan, then Camus introduces the point of reference, the original model into his novel in order to destroy it. Clamence transcends Don Juan's eighteenth century libertin-

ism when he proposes this ideal: "Ne m'aime pas et sois-moi
fidèle" (TRN, 1507). It appears that a woman's love, even if not
reciprocated, is a constraint on his freedom. Since most women,
however, are unwilling to submit to such a contract, Clamence
proposes a solution that privately tormented Camus: "Je me di-
sais . . . que la solution idéale eût été la mort pour la personne
qui m'intéressait. Cette mort eût définitivement fixé notre lien,
d'une part, et, de l'autre, lui eût ôté sa contrainte" (TRN, 1510).
These remarks can be traced as far back as 1943 to this entry in
the *Carnets*:

> La mort donne sa forme à l'amour comme elle la donne à la vie—le
> transformant en destin. Celle que tu aimes est morte dans le temps où
> tu l'aimais et voici desormais un amour fixé pour toujours—qui, sans
> cette fin, se serait désagrégé. Que serait ainsi le monde sans la mort, une
> suite de formes évanouissantes et renaissantes, une fuite angoissé, un
> monde inachevable. Mais heureusement la voici, elle, la stable. (C, 2,
> 90)

The cast of characters is different from Clamence's scenario because death is the third party consecrating the union of two
lovers. The Resistant and author of *Le Mythe de Sisyphe* wanted to
extend his political code to include the emotions and he argued
for a heroic love. Death for the beloved, like death for the conqueror, would continue to perform its essential task by absolving
both from the all too human decay that time inevitably brings.[11]
In *La Chute*, on the other hand, three become two as Clamence
performs the role of death, killing, in his imagination, a woman
he in fact does not love at all and whose death would consecrate
only her slavish fidelity. In 1951 Camus made this private confession: "Mon paradis était dans la virginité des autres" (C, 2,
341). Clamence amplifies this same remark:

> Je maintenais toutes mes affections autour de moi pour m'en servir
> quand je le voulais. Je ne pouvais donc vivre, de mon aveu même, qu'à
> la condition que, sur toute la terre, tous les êtres, ou le plus grand

---

11. More cynically Camus will write in *Le Mythe de Sisyphe*: "Il n'y a d'amour
éternel que contrarié" (E, 154).

nombre possible, fussent tournés vers moi, éternellement vacants, privés de vie indépendante . . . voués enfin à la stérilité. (TRN, 1510)

As long as Clamence's women remained in a state of suspended animation, he could sustain the illusion of libertine love. When a woman dies, however, Clamence's murderous nature is exposed. Camus is admitting that all the systems he proposed with regards to love, absurdist, heroic, or otherwise, were sophisticated justifications for aggression.[12] Camus made this admission intellectually in his study of Sade in *L'Homme révolté*, more intimately in *La Chute* in his portrayal of Clamence.

It is evident, moreover, that there is a strong bond between this aggressive misogyny and Camus' idealization of the fraternity of men. I have already suggested that Camus, between 1937 and 1944, considered male associations, particularly in sports, journalism, and politics, the appropriate means to his personal fulfillment. He wanted to achieve manhood in the competitive fraternity of warriors and writers. Because, for Camus, true friendship existed only between men, drawing its strength from the disciplines of intellect and liberty, it became the supreme virtue. The purpose of friendship and fraternity was, in turn, to create a new political order. To the extent that a woman incarnated biological continuity and, in that sense, an evolutionary concept of politics, she was an obstacle to the proposals Camus made in *Caligula*, *L'Etranger*, and *Le Mythe de Sisyphe* for our emancipation from the human condition. Radical history was apparently conceived in opposition to the woman and, by extension, to nature. The prerequisite for political progress, we observed in *Le Mythe de Sisyphe*, was biological sterility.

The Resistance and the post-war revolutionary fervor in France sustained Camus awhile in these beliefs. By *La Peste*, however, the fraternity that had resisted the Nazi plague now embodied the plague. The fraternity, valid when the association of men was spontaneous when, like the Resistance, it condensed the many impassioned responses to oppression into one voice, became corrupt when it survived the danger that called it into

12. Referring to a woman's fidelity, Camus wrote: "Sûr de sa fidélité et de sa stérilité absolue" (C, 2, 330).

being. The relative absence of women then changed from a present reality to an ideal requirement for the future, for a new world where, as Camus eventually admitted, man was supposed to be born from man:

> L'idéologie du XIXe siècle, du moins dans celles de ses tendances qui règnent aujourd'hui sur l'intelligence européenne, s'est détournée du rêve de Goethe unissant, avec Faust et Hélène, le titanisme contemporain et la beauté antique, et leur donnant un fils Euphorion. Le Faust contemporain a voulu ensuite avoir Euphorion sans Hélène, dans une sorte de délectation morose et orgueilleuse. Mais il n'a pu enfanter qu'un monstre de laboratoire au lieu de l'enfant merveilleux. Faust . . . pour être et créer, ne pouvait se passer d'Hélène. (E, 1710–11)

To bypass the woman was to substitute a political miracle for biological reality. The elimination of women from Utopia, however, once an ideal, is now, in the person of Clamence, a perversion. Clamence's repeated use of "cher," his desire to hold his listener's hand, his entire manner, are certainly homosexual. As a young man, Camus had written: "Il n'y a pas de limites pour aimer et que m'importe de mal étreindre si je peux tout embrasser" (E, 45). The notion of indiscriminate loving (or being loved indiscriminately) apparently did not lead Camus, at this time in his life, to ask whether a man is also a woman, whether a man can love another man. Nor had it yet occurred to him that sexual plenitude can destroy the living. The chart of human limitations and values that we normally carry with us was evidently unreliable, if not irrelevant. Human desire is certainly acknowledged in this passage but 'all' is the goal of a god. The woman, however, still remains the messenger from reality because physical distinctions occur in her presence. Clamence, Camus' contemporary Faust, who wishes to assume the roles of male and female, to incorporate the whole, ends up as a seducer of men and, pressing still further toward autonomy, ultimately his own lover.

As early as 1946 we hear Camus saying: "Je n'ai pas envie d'être un génie philosophique. Je n'ai même pas envie d'être un génie du tout, ayant déjà bien du mal à être un homme" (E, 1612). Thereafter, man, and not god, becomes the true measure of what is and is not possible. Camus will rarely miss an opportunity to contradict ideals he once cherished: "J'avoue, pour ma part, que je ne puis aimer l'humanité entière, sinon d'un amour vaste et un peu abstrait" (E, 1813); "On ne peut être aimé par tout le monde" (E, 1746). It is in his preface to the second edition of *L'Envers et l'endroit*, however, that Camus, reviewing his career, made what became his final accounting:

Depuis le temps où ces pages ont été écrites, j'ai vieilli et traversé beaucoup de choses. J'ai appris sur moi-même, connaissant mes limites, et presque toutes mes faiblesses. J'ai moins appris sur les êtres parce que ma curiosité va plus à leur destin qu'à leurs réactions et que les destins se répètent beaucoup. J'ai appris du moins qu'ils existaient et que l'égoisme, s'il ne peut se renier, doit essayer d'être clairvoyant. Jouir de soi est impossible; je le sais, malgré les grands dons qui sont les miens pour cet exercice. (E, 10)

Camus has revised his view of himself down to a more realistic scale. Such a revision no longer permits the absolute separation between the races of gods and men. It is the limited and unresolved qualities of a human nature that Camus wishes to emphasize for his reader, that rediscovery of character that Clamence rejects. What had once been a vision of a man's infinite potential, a compendium of rebirths and miracles, is now viewed by Camus, especially in *La Chute*, as a pathological and dangerous refusal to accept reality in any of its concrete forms. Camus had summarized, but in general philosophical terms, the results of his own self-analysis in *L'Homme révolté*: "Il s'agit de ne plus être, soit en refusant d'être quoi que ce soit, soit en acceptant d'être n'importe quoi" (E, 496). This book was still not personal enough. He decided to reedit *L'Envers et l'endroit*, to write *L'Exil et le royaume* with its many well-defined characters, and to create Jean-Baptiste Clamence who, rather than integrate himself in the kingdom of man, decided to be "anything at all" which is the same as being everything. And "everything," Camus concluded, is simply a prestigious synonym for "nothing."

Compared to Camus' other works *L'Exil et le royaume* has suffered considerable neglect. Its publication in 1957, one year after *La Chute*, went relatively unnoticed, partly because Camus' "silence" during the Algerian crisis, especially his refusal to support terrorist activities, made him an unpopular figure among French intellectuals, partly because these short stories were unlike anything he had written before.[13]

For the first time Camus dedicated a work to a woman, his wife, and two of the six stories deal with intimate, domestic crises: Janine in *La Femme adultère*, faced with impending old age, tries to sort out her feelings about her husband whom she may love or simply need for emotional support or both; in *Jonas* a successful painter wants to reconcile his art with the necessary demands of his family and public. Expanding his field of vision, Camus evokes with uncommon realism the life of Yvars and other workers, who, having struck unsuccessfully, are trying desperately to earn a living and maintain their dignity.

The other stories offer direct and corrective comments on works Camus had already published. The missionary in *Le Renégat* dreams of a political Utopia of hate because he thinks that hate, unlike love, is monolithic and pure. His internal monologue resembles Clamence's but stripped of the latter's wit and self-mockery. Unable to speak, his tongue torn out by natives, he becomes his own echo chamber, an image of impotence as he eats his own words. In *L'Hôte* Daru must decide whether or not to give his Arab prisoner over to the authorities. The Arab was a blur to Meursault but now we read: "Il fallait regarder cet homme" (TRN, 1618–19). A native vows to carry an enormous rock during a religious procession in *La Pierre qui pousse* and, collapsing under its weight, is aided by the principal character, D'Arrast, who then carries the burden not to the church but to the native's home. Sisyphus is no longer alone and the human condition includes the human community.

Although Camus had created characters such as Meursault, Tarrou, and Clamence who embodied attitudes toward life that were outlined sharply, he is now willing to be less systematic, to describe his characters in greater physical detail and place them

---

13. Peter Cryle has written a detailed and useful analysis of critical reaction to these stories: *L'Exil et le royaume d'Albert Camus* (Paris: Lettres Modernes, 1973).

in three dimensional space. This "physical realism," as Peter Cryle calls it in his valuable study of the stories,[14] underlines their moral confusion. Integrated into physical and social worlds, characters such as Daru, D'Arrast, Janine, Jonas, and Yvars are caught in dilemmas which are never resolved.

The earlier manuscripts of these stories included many commentaries of a general nature, frames of reference that Camus himself provided. The characters would again be contained by the author's argument.[15] Camus then deleted these passages. He was evidently more willing to enter into the subjective lives of his characters. As he explained in his preface to *L'Envers et l'endroit*, this procedure involved certain risks:

> Pour être édifiée, l'oeuvre d'art doit se servir d'abord de ces forces obscures de l'âme. Mais non sans les canaliser, les entourer de digues, pour que leur flot monte, aussi bien. Mes digues, aujourd'hui encore, sont peut-être trop hautes. De là, cette raideur, parfois. . . . Simplement, le jour où l'équilibre s'établira entre ce que je suis et ce que je dis, ce jour-là peut-être, et j'ose à peine l'écrire, je pourrai bâtir l'oeuvre dont je rêve. . . . Ce que j'ai voulu dire ici, c'est qu'elle . . . parlera d'une certaine forme d'amour. (E, 12)

One might well ask whether there can ever be such an equilibrium, whether it is the search for equilibrium that in fact is translated into each text and there temporarily satisfied. Camus' works have that balance between form and content but now he brings up the question of depth. Evidently, to loosen his grip on his characters, to remove those all-enveloping, intellectual, and perhaps protective generalizations meant tapping the unconscious, the "obscure forces of the soul," more than he had ever done before. This preface itself was a step in that direction. Twice he refers to his indifference, calling it "naturelle" (E, 6) or "une infirmité de nature" (E, 10), as if to give the lie to his youthful statements "Je veux être indifférent." Although he strongly suspected even then that he resembled his mother, he thought

14. Ibid., p. 16.
15. Ibid., p. 46.

he would invent his nature. Having accepted what he is, the dikes were beginning to lower. Characters, drawn from the deeper recesses of his soul, would be allowed to speak for themselves.

The unfinished manuscript of *Le Premier homme* also offers conclusive evidence that Camus' premature death has distorted the final shape of his work.[16] Clamence does not have the last word. This man with no biography was to have been surpassed by the protagonist of an autobiographical novel. The pure invention of one man with his single voice, his highly selective and manipulative style, coexisted with a text that would follow the broken and cumulative curves of a man's inhabited life. Here too the novelist would select his memories but out of excess. This long manuscript, rich in memories Camus once thought inappropriate even to confessions, detailed memories he released partially in *L'Exil et le royaume*, would have been, in his own words, his first novel. It would have been a novel in the sense of holding within its borders a pluralistic, satisfyingly populated universe which the reader could hold in his hand.

It was entirely appropriate that in 1955 Roger Martin du Gard, a "traditional" novelist, asked Camus to write the preface to his collected works.[17] As Camus examines *Devenir* and *Les Thibault*, he appreciates what he calls the ambiguity of the characters (E, 1136) through which we reinterpret our own lives. That ambiguity contrasts with the duplicity of Clamence, a trait that is meant to protect the speaker and victimize the listener. The essay on Martin du Gard defines the kind of writer Camus wanted to be and was becoming at the time of his fatal accident: "Martin du Gard partage avec Tolstoï le goût des êtres, l'art de les peindre dans leur obscurité charnelle. . . . Nos écrivains . . . gardent l'espoir, même s'ils ne l'avouent pas, de retrouver les secrets d'un art universel qui, à force d'humilité et de maîtrise, ressusciterait enfin les personnages dans leur chair et leur durée" (E, 1132).

A pluralistic vision makes the artist a citizen. It places both in

---

16. We do not forget that what we have is only a first draft of Camus' last novel.

17. E, 1915.

a demanding and unharmonious social space because they are both pulled and prodded by duties and desires. In his acceptance speech for the Nobel prize, in interviews and lectures, we hear Camus taking various soundings of his multiple and contradictory loyalties. He was convinced that the modern sickness grew out of the various cures offered for the human condition when there was nothing else but the human condition. Camus sensed that a totalitarian century had created an art in its image and that he was included in that image if for no other reason that his characters, so few, followed their author perhaps too systematically, too slavishly. In Camus' own terms, they did not lie enough. Roger Quilliot had many conversations with Camus who was aware at this time of undergoing a profound transition and he summarized Camus' state of mind:

Il s'inquiète du moralisme qu'on lui reproche. Ce genre de critique l'exaspère dans la mesure où il en sent la justesse partielle. On l'a fait passer pour vertueux. Il est fatigué de cette réputation. Certes, il est honnête homme et n'abuse de la confiance de personne. Mais il n'aime pas la vertu pour elle-même. Le plus souvent, il n'est vertueux que par orgueil, non par devoir. La vertu fut pour lui la suite logique de la Résistance, "une explosion vertueuse." Alors, il a fallu juger, classer, opposer bien et mal. Il est las du manichéisme et préférerait retrouver la complexité de l'existence. Telle serait d'ailleurs la ligne de son nouvel essai: partir des valeurs etablies par la révolte, et, après s'être élevé aux conséquences logiques, les confronter à l'expérience concrète, les diluer dans la richesse sensuelle de la vie quotidienne. (TRN, 2038)

That sensual richness of everyday life which the greatest novelists offer was, for Camus, inextricably linked to his origins, and Camus made his greatest pilgrimage to those sources in *L'Exil et le royaume* and in his last, unfinished novel. Of course, origins themselves could never exhaust the possibilities of the novel but they represented for Camus the at least partial consent the writer must give to what he is in order to respond fully and critically to experiences and their resonance.

Le Premier homme begins with a description of a woman in labor, Camus' mother, and the story Camus is telling precedes his own birth. The recognition of predecessors helps to erase the imperial vision altogether because that recognition derives its power from the organic cycles of life, not from miracles. We are born, as it were, already inhabited. It also becomes evident that Camus' description of the husband and wife who are far from the nearest village and are anxiously seeking some kind of lodging was traced over the story of Christ's birth. The title, however, anchors the story in the creation of a man.

When Camus died he left behind an unfinished novel, a work through which he hoped to make the transition to a new art based on a new (and very old) vision of self. His death does not distort the early works, *L'Etranger* and *Le Mythe de Sisyphe*, or even those of the second cycle, *La Peste* and *L'Homme révolté*. Without *Le Premier homme*, however, *L'Exil et le royaume* and *La Chute*, while complete as works of art, remain unfinished chapters of an extraordinary life. Camus, alas, is dead. Nevertheless, he earned a compliment he would no longer have disdained. He was a man.

Bibliography
Index

Bibliography

Works by Camus

Carnets, mai 1935–février 1942. Paris: Gallimard, 1962.

Carnets, janvier 1942–mars 1951. Paris: Gallimard, 1964.

Ecrits de jeunesse d'Albert Camus in *Le Premier Camus*, Paul Viallaneix, *Cahiers Albert Camus*, 2. Mayenne: Gallimard, 1973.

Essais. Roger Quilliot and L. Faucon, eds. Bruges: Gallimard, 1965.

Journaux de voyages. Mayenne: Gallimard, 1978.

La Mort heureuse, *Cahiers Albert Camus*, 1, Jean Sarocchi, ed. Paris: Gallimard, 1971.

Théâtre, Récits, Nouvelles. Roger Quilliot, ed. Bruges: Gallimard, 1962.

Works Consulted

Anderson, Quentin. *The Imperial Self*. New York: Knopf, 1971.

Archambault, Paul. *Camus' Hellenic Sources*. Chapel Hill: University of North Carolina Press, 1972.

Barnes, Hazel E. *The Literature of Possibility. A Study in Humanistic Existentialism.* London: Tavistock Publications, 1961.

Barchilón, José. "A Study of Camus' Mythopoeic Tale *The Fall*," *Journal of the American Psychoanalytic Association* 19, no. 2 (April 1971): 193–240.

Barrier, Maurice George. *L'Art du récit dans "L'Etranger" d'Albert Camus.* Paris: Nizet, 1966.

Barthes, Roland. "*L'Etranger*, roman solaire," *Club (Bulletin du Club du Meilleur Livre)*, no. 12 (April 1954), p. 7.

Bernard, Jacqueline. "The Background of *The Plague*. Albert Camus' Experience in the French Resistance," *Kentucky Romance Quarterly*, no. 2 (1967), pp. 165–73.

Bersani, Leo. "The Stranger's Secrets," *Novel* 3, no. 3 (Spring 1970): 212–24.

Bespaloff, Rachel. "Le Monde du condamné à mort," *Esprit*, no. 163 (January 1950), pp. 1–26.

Bieber, Konrad. "*Engagement* as a Professional Risk," *Yale French Studies* 16 (Winter 1955): 29–39.

———. "The Rebellion of a Humanist (*L'Homme révolté*)," *The Yale Review*, no. 3 (Spring 1954), pp. 473–75.

Bloch-Michel, Jean. "Albert Camus et la nostalgie d'innocence" *Preuves*. no. 110 (1960), pp. 3–9.

Bonnier, Henry. *Albert Camus ou la force d'être.* Lyon-Paris: Vitte, 1959.

Brady, Patrick. "Manifestations of Eros and Thanatos in *L'Etranger*," *Twentieth Century Literature* 20 (July 1974): 183–88.

Braun, Lev. *Witness of Decline. Albert Camus, Moralist of the Absurd.* Rutherford: Fairleigh Dickinson Press, 1974.

Brearley, Katherine. "The Theme of Isolation in Camus," *Kentucky French Language Quarterly* 9 (1962): 117–22.

Brée, Germaine. *Albert Camus.* New York: Columbia University Press, 1964.

———. *Camus*, rev. ed. New Brunswick: Rutgers University Press, 1972.

———. *Camus and Sartre: Crisis and Commitment.* New York: Delacorte Press, 1972.

———, ed. *Camus; A Collection of Critical Essays.* Englewood Cliffs: Prentice-Hall, 1962.

Brisville, Jean-Claude. *Camus.* Paris: Gallimard, 1959.

Brochier, Jean Jacques. *Albert Camus, philosophe pour classes terminales.* Paris: André Balland, 1970.

Brombert, Victor. *The Intellectual Hero.* Philadelphia: Lippincott, 1961.

Burton, Arthur. "Schizophrenia and Existence," *Psychology: Journal for the Study of Interpersonal Processes* 23, no. 4 (Nov. 1960): 385–94.

Bychowski, Gustav. "The Archaic Object and Alienation," *The International Journal of Psycho-Analysis* 43 (1967): 384–93.

Carruth, Hayden. *After the Stranger. Imaginary Dialogue with Camus.* New York: Macmillan, 1965.

Castex, Pierre-George. *Albert Camus et "L'Etranger."* Paris: Corte, 1965.

Champigny, Robert. "Camus' Fictional Works: The Plight of Innocence," *American Society of the Legion of Honor Magazine* 28 (1957): 173–82.

———. *Humanism and Human Racism: A Critical Study of Essays by Sartre and Camus.* The Hague: Mouton, 1972.

———. *Sur un héros païen.* Paris: Gallimard, 1959.

Clayton, Alan J. *Etapes d'un itinéraire spirituel, Albert Camus de 1937 à 1944.* Paris: Lettres Modernes, 1971.

Coombs, Ilona. *Camus, homme de théâtre.* Paris: Nizet, 1968.

Costes, Alain. *Albert Camus ou la parole manquante; étude psychanalytique.* Paris: Payot, 1973.

Courrière, Yves. *Le Temps des léopards, La Guerre d'Algérie,* vol. 2. Fayard, 1969. Contains five previously unpublished letters of Camus to Charles Poncet in Algeria.

Crochet, Monique. *Les Mythes dans l'oeuvre de Camus.* Paris: Editions Universitaires, 1973.

Cruickshank, John. *Albert Camus and the Literature of Revolt.* London. Oxford University Press, 1960.

———. "The Art of Allegory in *La Peste,*" *Symposium* 11, no. 1 (Spring 1957): 61–74.

————. "Camus' Technique in *L'Etranger*," *French Studies* 10, no. 3 (July 1956):241–53.

Cryle, Peter. *L'Exil et le royaume d'Albert Camus*. Paris: Lettres Modernes, 1973.

Curtis, Jerry L. "Meursault or the Leap of Death," *Rice University Studies* 2 (1971):41–48.

————. "Camus' Vision of Greatness," *Orbis Literarum* 29 (1974): 338–54.

Dennis, William, D. "Jean-Baptiste Clamence—A Resurrected Meursault?" *College Language Association Journal* 8 (1964):81–87.

Durand, Anne. *Le Cas Albert Camus*. Paris: Editions Fischbacher, 1961.

Engleberg, Edward. *The Unknown Distance: From Consciousness to Conscience. Goethe to Camus*. Cambridge: Harvard University Press, 1972.

Falk, Eugene H. *Types of Thematic Structure: The Nature and Function of Motifs in Gide, Camus, and Sartre*. Chicago: University of Chicago Press, 1967.

Fitch, Brian T., ed. *Albert Camus*, 1–6, 8. Paris: Minard, 1968–78.

————. "Aesthetic Distance and Inner Space in the Novels of Camus," *Modern Fiction Studies* 10, no. 3 (Autumn 1964):279–92.

————. *L'Etranger d'Albert Camus: un texte, ses lecteurs, leurs lectures*. Paris: Librarie Larousse, 1972.

————. *Narrateur et narration dans "L'Etranger" d'Albert Camus*. Paris: Lettres Modernes, 1970.

————. *Le Sentiment d'étrangeté chez Malraux, Sartre, Camus, et S. de Beauvoir*. Paris: Minard, 1964.

————. "Le Statut précaire du personnage et de l'univers romanesques chez Camus," *Symposium* 24, no. 3 (Fall 1970):218–28.

Fletcher, John. *"Interpreting* L'Etranger," *The French Review* 43, no. 1 (Winter 1970):158–67.

————. "Meursault's Rhetoric," *Critical Quarterly* 13 (Summer 1971): 125–36.

Freeman, Edward. *The Theatre of Albert Camus: A Critical Study*. London: Methuen, 1971.

Frohock, W. M. "Image, Influence, and Sensibility," *Style and Temper. Studies in French Fiction.* Cambridge: Harvard University Press, 1967, pp. 103–15.

Gadourek, Carina. *Les Innocents et les coupables; Essai d'exégèse de l'oeuvre d'Albert Camus.* La Haye: Mouton, 1963.

Gagnebin, Laurent. *Albert Camus dans sa lumière; Essai sur l'évolution de sa pensée.* Lausanne: Cahiers de la Renaissance Vaudoise, 1964.

Gaillard, Pol. *Albert Camus.* Paris: Bordas, 1973.

Gay-Crosior, Raymond, ed. *Albert Camus*, vol. 7. Paris: Minard, 1957.

———. "L'anarchisme mesuré de Camus," *Symposium* 24, no. 3 (Fall 1970):243–53.

———. "Camus et le Donjuanisme," *French Review* 41 (May 1968): 818–30.

———. *Les Envers d'un échec. Etude sur le théâtre d'Albert Camus.* Paris: Minard, 1967.

Geerts, W. "Sur le 'soleil' dans *L'Etranger.* Psychocritique et analyse formelle," *Revue Romane*, no. 8 (1973), pp. 406–7.

Gélinas, Germain Paul. *La Liberté dans la pensée d'Albert Camus.* Fribourg: Editions Universitaires, 1965.

Ginestier, Paul. *La Pensée de Camus.* Paris: Bordas, 1964.

Girard, René. "*Camus' Stranger Retried,*" *PMLA* 79 (December 1964): 519–33.

Goedert, Georges. *Albert Camus et la question du bonheur.* Luxembourg: Edi-Centre, 1969.

Grenier, Jean. *Albert Camus, souvenirs.* Paris: Gallimard, 1968.

Hanna, Thomas. *The Lyrical Existentialists.* New York: Atheneum, 1962.

———. *The Thought and Art of Albert Camus.* Chicago: H. Regnery Co., 1958.

Hardstock, Mildred. "Camus' *The Fall.* Dialogue of One," *Modern Fiction Studies* 7 (1961):357–64.

Hewitt, Nicholas. "*La Chute* and *Les Temps Modernes,*" *Essays in French Literature*, no. 10 (1973), pp. 64–81.

Hommage à Albert Camus. Paris: Gallimard, 1967.

Hugo, Victor. "Préface," *Les Contemplations*. Bourges: Garnier, 1957.

Jacobi, Finn. "La Métamorphose de Meursault. Une interprétation du premier chapitre de *L'Etranger* de Camus," *Revue Romane* 4 (1969): 138–47.

Jeanson, Francis. "Albert Camus ou l'âme révoltée," *Les Temps Modernes*, no. 79 (May 1952): 2070–90.

———. "Pour tout vous dire," *Les Temps modernes*, no. 83 (August 1952), pp. 354–83.

Johnson, Patricia J. "A Further Source for Camus' *L'Etranger*," *Romance Notes* 2 (1970): 465–68.

Johnson, Robert B. "Camus' *La Chute* or Montherlant s'éloigne," *French Review* 44 (May 1971): 1026–32.

Kellogg, Jean Defrees. *Dark Prophets of Hope—Dostoevsky, Sartre, Camus, Faulkner*. Chicago: Loyola University Press, 1975.

King, Adele. *Camus*. Edinburg and London: Oliver and Boyd, 1964.

Kirk, Irina. *Dostoevsky and Camus*. München: Fink, 1974.

Kirk, Russell. *Enemies of the Permanent Things. Observations of Abnormality in Literature and Politics*. New Rochelle: Arlington House, 1969.

Knoff, William F. "A Psychiatrist Reads Camus' *The Stranger*," *Psychiatric Opinion*, (1969): 19–21, 24.

Lazère, Donald. *The Unique Creation of Albert Camus*. New Haven: Yale University Press, 1973.

Lebesque, Morvan. *Camus par lui-même*. Paris: Editions du Seuil, 1965.

Leclerq, P. R. *Rencontres avec Camus*. Paris: L'Ecole, 1970.

Levi-Valensi, Jacqueline, ed. *Les Critiques de notre temps et Camus*. Paris: Garnier, 1970.

Lottman, Herbert R. *Albert Camus*. Garden City: Doubleday, 1979.

Luppé, Robert de. *Albert Camus*. Editions Universitaires, 1952.

Mailhot, Laurent. *Albert Camus ou L'Imagination du désert*. Montréal: Presses de l'Université de Montréal, 1973.

Majault, Joseph. *Camus, révolte et liberté*. Paris: Editions du Centurion, 1965.

Manly, William M. "Journey to Consciousness: the Symbolic Pattern of Camus's *L'Etranger*," *PMLA* 79, no. 3 (June 1964): 321–28.

Maquet, Albert. *Albert Camus ou L'Invincible été.* Paris: Nouvelles Editions Debresse, 1956.

Massey, Irving. *The Uncreating Word; Romanticism and the Object.* Bloomington: Indiana University Press, 1970.

Masters, Brian. *Camus, a Study.* Totowa: Rowman and Littlefield, 1974.

Matthews, J. H., ed. *Configuration Critique d'Albert Camus: Camus devant la critique anglo-saxonne*, vol. 1. Paris: Minard, 1962.

Merton, Thomas. *Albert Camus' The Plague.* New York: Seabury Press, 1968.

Musset, Alfred de. *Lorenzaccio. Comédies et proverbes*, vol. 1. Paris: Garnier, 1960.

Nguyen Van-Huy, Pierre. *La Métaphysique du bonheur chez Albert Camus.* Neuchâtel: La Baconnière, 1962.

————. Phan Thi Ngoc, Mai, avec la collaboration de Jean-René Peltier. *La Chute de Camus: ou, Le Dernier testament: étude du message camusien de responsabilité et d'authenticité selon La Chute.* Neuchâtel: La Baconnière, 1974.

Nicolas, André. *Albert Camus ou Le Vrai Prométhée.* Paris: Séghers, 1966.

————. *Une Philosophie de l'existence: Albert Camus.* Paris: Presses Universitaires de France, 1964.

Nuttall, A. D. "Did Meursault Mean to Kill the Arab? The Intentional Fallacy Fallacy," *The Critical Quarterly* 10, nos. 1–2 (Spring–Summer 1968): 95–106.

O'Brien, Conor Cruise. *Albert Camus of Europe and Africa.* New York: Viking Press, 1970.

Onimus, Jean. *Camus*, 3rd ed. Paris: Desclée de Brouwer, 1966.

Parker, Emmett. *Albert Camus. The Artist in the Arena.* Madison: University of Wisconsin Press, 1965.

Patri, A. "Note sur un sentiment d'étrangeté," *L'Arche* 2, no. 5 (August September 1944): 115 17

Pichon-Rivière, Arminda A. de; Baranger, Willy. "Répression du deuil et intensification des mécanismes et des angoisses schizo-paranoïdes (notes sur *L'Etranger* de Camus)," *Revue Française de Psychanalyse* 23, (May–June 1959): 409–20.

Pinnoy, M. *Albert Camus*. Paris: Desclée de Brouwer, 1961.

Quilliot, Roger. "Camus—*L'Exil et le royaume*," *La Revue Socialiste*, no. 109 (July, 1957), pp. 217–18.

———. *La Mer et les prisons. Essai sur Albert Camus*. Paris: Gallimard, 1956.

———. "Un Monde ambigu," *Preuves*, no. 110 (April, 1960), 28–38.

———. *L'Univers théâtral et romanesque d'Albert Camus*. Rodez: Subervie, 1964.

Redfern, W. D. "The Prisoners of Stendhal and Camus," *French Review* 41 (April 1968):649–59.

Rey, Pierre-Louis. *Camus. La Chute*. Paris: Hatier, 1970.

———. *Camus. L'Etranger*. Paris: Hatier, 1970.

Rhein, Phillip. *Albert Camus*. New York: Twayne, 1969.

Roeming, Robert F. "The Concept of the Judge-Penitent of Albert Camus," *Transcript of the Wisconsin Academy of Science, Arts, and Letters* 48 (1960):143–49.

Ross, Stephen. *Literature and Philosophy. An Analysis of the Philosophical Novel*. New York: Appleton-Century Crofts, 1969.

Rossi, Louis, R. "Albert Camus: The Plague of Absurdity," *The Kenyon Review* 20, no. 3 (Summer 1958):399–422.

Rysten, Felix. *False Prophets in the Fiction of Camus, Dostoevsky, Melville, and Others*. Coral Gables: University of Miami Press, 1972.

Sarocchi, Jean. *Camus*. Paris: Presses Universitaires de Paris, 1968.

Sartre, Jean Paul. *La Nausée*. Paris: Gallimard, 1970.

———. "Explication de *L'Etranger*," *Situations*, 1. Paris: Gallimard, 1947.

———. "Réponse à Albert Camus," *Situations*, 4. Paris: Gallimard, 1964.

Scott, Nathan A. *Albert Camus*. New York: Hillary House Publishers, 1962.

Shattuck, Roger. "Two Inside Narratives: *Billy Budd* and *L'Etranger*," *Texas Studies in Literature and Language* 4 (1962):314–20.

Simon, Pierre-Henri. *L'Homme en procès. Malraux, Sartre, Camus, Saint-Exupéry*. Paris: Petite Bibliothèque Payot, 1965.

———. *Présence de Camus*. Bruxelles: Renaissance du Livre, 1961.

Slochower, Harry. "Camus' *The Stranger*: the Silent Society and the Ecstasy of Rage," *American Imago* 26, no. 3 (Fall 1969): 291–94.

Smith, Albert B. "Eden as Symbol in Camus' *L'Etranger*," *Romance Notes* 9, no. 1 (Autumn 1967: 1–5.

Sperber, Michael A. "Camus' *The Fall*. The Icarus Complex," *American Imago* 26, no. 3 (Fall 1969): 269–80.

————. "Symptoms and Structures of Borderline Personality Organization," *Literature and Psychology* 23, no. 3 (1973): 102–13.

Stamm, Julian L. "Camus' *Stranger*: His Act Of Violence," *American Imago* 26, no. 3 (Fall 1969): 281–90.

Stokle, Norman. *Le Combat d'Albert Camus*. Quebec: Presses de L'Université Laval, 1970.

Sugden, Leonard W. "Meursault, an Oriental Sage," *French Review* 6 (1974): 196–207.

Thieberger, R., ed. *Configuration Critique d'Albert Camus: Camus devant la critique de langue allemande*, vol. 2. Paris: Minard, 1963.

Thody, Philip. *Albert Camus; A Study of His Work*. London: H. Hamilton, 1957.

————. *Albert Camus, 1913–1960*. New York: Macmillan, 1962.

————. "Meursault et la critique," *La Revue des Lettres Modernes* 8, nos. 64–66 (Autumn 1961), 11–23.

Treil, Claude. *L'Indifférence dans l'oeuvre d'Albert Camus*. Sherbrooke: Editions Cosmos, 1971.

Tucker, Warren. "*La Chute*: voie du salut terrestre," *The French Review* 43, no. 5 (April 1970): 737–44.

Viallaneix, Paul. *Le Premier Camus, suivi de Ecrits de jeunesse d'Albert Camus. Cahiers Albert Camus 2*, Mayenne: Gallimard, 1973.

Viggiani, Carl A. "Camus' *L'Etranger*," *PMLA* 71, no. 3 (1956): 865–87.

————. "Camus and the Fall from Innocence," *Yale French Studies*, no. 25 (Spring 1960), pp. 65–71.

Wagner, Robert C. "The Silence of *The Stranger*," *Modern Fiction Studies* 16, no. 1 (Spring 1970): 27–40.

Wasserstrom, William. "In Gertrude's Closet," *Yale Review* 48 (1958), 245–65.

Werner, Eric. *De la violence au totalitarisme; Essai sur la pensée de Camus et de Sartre*. Paris: Calmann-Lévy, 1972.

Willhoite, Fred H. *Beyond Nihilism; Albert Camus's Contribution to Political Thought*. Baton Rouge: Louisiana State University Press, 1968.

Woelfel, James W. *Camus: A Theological Perspective*. Nashville: Abingdon Press, 1975.

Zants, Emily. "Camus's Deserts and Their Allies, Kingdoms of the Stranger," *Symposium* 17 (1963): 30–41.